A Lodge at Labor
Freemasons and Masonry Today

A Cornerstone Book

A Lodge at Labor
Freemasons and Masonry Today
by Michael R. Poll

A Cornerstone Book
Published by Cornerstone Book Publishers
Copyright © 2019, 2022, 2023 by Michael R. Poll

Cornerstone Book Publishers
Hot Springs Village, AR

First Cornerstone Edition – 2019
Second Cornerstone Edition – 2022
Third Cornerstone Edition - 2023

www.cornerstonepublishers.com

Table of Contents

Introduction

In the days of the old Operative Freemasons, a lodge at labor meant a company of workers in the building trade at work on a job. The old Operatives were builders who were hired to erect everything from magnificent cathedrals from the ground up to remodeling an existing structure. They were called *free* masons because they were not bondsmen or slaves; they were free to travel anywhere to accept work. When a *lodge* (a group of builders hired for a job) was *at labor*, it meant that they were working on a construction project. For an Operative Freemason, the term is rather straightforward in its meaning.

But what does *a lodge at labor* mean to the Speculative Freemason? We are not actual builders — at least, not with stone, steel, or wood. We often say that our *building* is internal — we take that which is less and make it better than it was before. We are *at labor* to make ourselves better human beings. That sounds noble and most inviting, but it does not answer the question. What exactly is *a lodge at labor*? Are we talking about a business meeting? If so, what do we do during a business meeting? Do we work towards that noble goal, or do we read the minutes, pay bills, and talk about an upcoming social event? Really, what is it that we do at lodge? What and where are the parts that make us better than we were before?

The goal of this book is simple — to provide a view of problems that we face in today's Freemasonry and offer opinions on solving these problems. Maybe also to take a bit of a look at history. We are always free to accept or reject whatever we wish. The one goal is to give a reason to stop and reconsider Freemasonry. It is far more than a social club. Once this is realized, then those who are willing can do what is needed to bring a new Age of Enlightenment to Freemasonry. We can elevate our lodges into centers of education designed to help us be more than we are and give us Light in a sometimes dark world. I believe that the Freemasonry that is deep within our teachings can return to be the shining Light for those who can or are willing to see it. I believe that by doing these things, *then* we are *a lodge at labor*.

Michael R. Poll
January 2019

A Lodge at Labor

Freemasons and Masonry Today

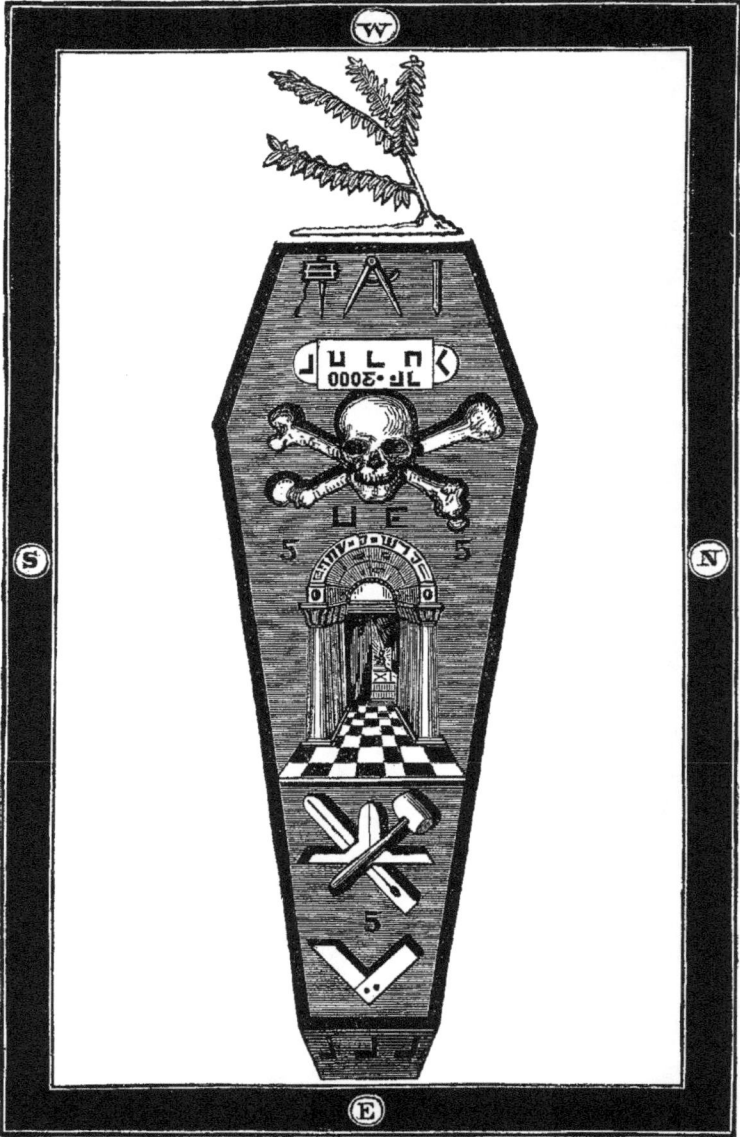

Freemasonry the Verb

I'd like to share a few thoughts. It is sometimes of value to stop for a moment and take a look at ourselves — the whole of Freemasonry. Who are we, what are we, and why is there a need for an organization like Freemasonry? One way to try and understand who and what we are is to go back to the past. I don't mean the early days of Speculative Freemasonry. I also don't mean to the days of the old Operative Freemasons. I mean to an earlier time. Let's go back to the Dark Ages.

The Dark Ages are known as a time of general ignorance and lack of development for most of Europe. The time was metaphorically dark in contrast to when people grew in light or enlightenment. People during this time were anything but enlightened. It was also a time of many plagues, diseases, and poverty. Death could come quickly at any time. We can only imagine the extraordinary struggle of daily life during this period.

There is a theory that the people's ignorance during the Dark Ages was not by their own choice but by a conceived plan. It's thought there was a policy by the kings, emperors, and maybe even the church to keep the masses ignorant. It may have been felt that an uneducated population was far easier to control than an educated one. That is a military tactic for dictators.

Free expression was not allowed during the Dark Ages. Education was not allowed. Voicing opinions, thoughts, or beliefs which were different from those who were in charge could result in imprisonment, or worse. There was only one thought, one opinion, or one belief that was allowed. That was the one held by whoever was in charge — the church, king, or emperor. If you had any opinion that was different from whoever was giving the orders, you would be wise to keep it to yourself. Only *one* opinion was allowed, and if you were on the bottom rung, you had better openly agree with the thoughts you were given.

One of the most recognizable symbols of Freemasonry today is the Bible. On the altars of our lodges, we find the Bible. When our lodges are at labor, we find the Bible open. We sometimes forget or don't think about the significance of the Bible being open on our altars. The simple fact is that you can't read a closed Bible. In order to read the Bible and know what's in it, you must open it. That is exactly what was *not permitted* during the Dark Ages. During that time, the Bible was not allowed to be read by those few who could read. You did not find a Bible open anywhere — except in church. If you wanted to know what was inside the Bible, you asked your priest. He would tell you what was inside the Bible. You would not be allowed to find that out for yourself. The reason would seem simple. If you read the Bible, you may understand it differently from the way that you were told. That was the last thing that was wanted. To control religion, you must control who reads the Bible.

It was a time that can be considered as *the time of one*. Only one thought, one opinion, and one belief was allowed. The only way to do things was the way that you were told to do them by whoever was in charge — the church, king, or emperor. Therefore, in defiance of *the time of one*, the Bible is open on our Masonic altars. The Bible is there for you to read, understand, and decide for yourself what it means.

During the Dark Ages, if you expressed an opinion or belief different than the one that was allowed, you went to prison or were executed. But while it was possible to control unwanted opinions and beliefs that were spoken, it was *not* possible to control or even know what someone was thinking. The policy of one could not affect the private thoughts of individuals.

There were no televisions, internet, or cell phones during the Dark Ages with which someone could find entertainment. The people lived a much simpler lifestyle. For entertainment, they often walked outside, sat under a tree, and thought about things. They would think about anything and everything. It was here that this policy of one began to fall apart.

Because there was no way to control what someone thought, individuals began to think about many things. They allowed their minds to wander and began to imagine new concepts and ideas. What are the stars? Why does the wind blow? When I feel ill, why do some plants help me? Why do I exist? On and on, the thoughts and private ideas came. Humans seek to know, and they will not be denied. Even with these academically limited people, basic concepts of mathematics, science, medicine, and many other complex disciplines were being thought about and explored.

Yet even with all sorts of wonderous ideas and thoughts filling their minds, they could still *act* like their only thought was the one given to them by whoever was in charge. The problem for the ones in charge was that they had no idea what others were thinking in their private thoughts. The problem for those thinking these wonderful new ideas was that they had no one with which to share them. These new ideas began to bubble up in the people, and since humans are social creatures, it became increasingly difficult to keep these secret thoughts to themselves. What happened next completely changed the world.

The people sitting around and thinking of beautiful ideas simply had to do something with them. They had to share these ideas to see if they were of any value. They wanted to test the ideas and put them into action. It would seem logical that when they did share their ideas, it would first be with a family member or close friend who they could trust. But it was inevitable that they would end up sharing their thoughts and ideas with someone.

Of course, when a private thought was shared, it would be explained that what they wanted to tell was a *secret*, and if the secrecy was violated, they could get in a great deal of trouble. The people may have been ignorant, but they were not stupid. They would tell the secret ideas to selected individuals, and then something amazing would often happen. Many times, the one being told the secret idea would return the favor and tell his own secret idea, maybe as payment for sharing with him.

So, where originally you had two people, each with one idea, now you have two people with two new ideas each. Both benefited from the sharing of ideas. That was a very important, desirable, and good thing for them both. But it didn't stop there.

After a while, little groups were formed. Maybe half a dozen or so individuals were sworn to secrecy. These little groups began telling their private thoughts and ideas to the group, and everyone benefited. They found this to be an extremely favorable arrangement. They were educating each other as well as allowing everyone to evaluate new ideas to discover their worth. They were very aware that what they were doing was against the law, but they were also aware that it was necessary for them to do this to grow as human beings. Little groups benefitted from each other since the beginning of time.

These little groups met in secret, taught each other in secret, and helped each other become better than they were before they joined the group. It was the distant seed that would one day grow into what we know today as Speculative Freemasonry. Of course, these details are pure speculation, but they are born out of logic and a study of human nature. Let's say that you see someone sitting in a chair. The next time you see him, he is standing outside. Based on these events, you can logically assume that, at some point, he got up and walked outside.

Make no mistake, what these little groups were doing in secret during the Dark Ages was precisely what is natural for humans to do. You cannot forcibly keep people ignorant forever. Our minds are private, and while we can be deceived and believe things that are just not so, we are mentally capable of eventually working out the truth. The growth of our minds will not be denied.

Little academic study groups, over time, eventually developed into Speculative Freemasonry via groups like the Royal Society of London. They were not entertainment clubs or social groups. They were individuals on an actual mission. They were doing something important for themselves as well as all humanity.

In those early days, Freemasonry, and the groups from which it evolved, were verbs — an action. Freemasonry was doing something. Look at our teachings and the times in which Speculative Freemasonry was born. It provided an education that was found nowhere else. Stop and think for a minute. You can get in your car today and drive down any street you choose. You will probably pass more than a few churches of all different faiths. They are all there, clearly identifying themselves with signs saying, "Here I am. This is what we teach. This is what we believe." They are not hiding. They are very much in the open. Children are today not denied education. It's just the opposite. Children are required *by law* to go to school and learn all the things that had been denied them during the Dark Ages.

Yes, we have many problems in this world. Our country is politically divided, but it is *free*. We will not be stood against a wall and executed simply because we express an opinion different from our leaders. We will not be imprisoned because we express a different religious belief. We will not get into trouble because we seek to learn or have ideas of science, medicine, or pretty much anything else that is different. We have a freedom today that those during the Dark Ages could scarcely imagine.

Very early Speculative Freemasonry was in an actual war against ignorance. In many areas, they met in secret because to be open about what they were doing and teaching would mean imprisonment. The work that they were doing was dead serious. They were teaching humanity by educating their members. They were giving their members the opportunity to grow, to learn, and to experience the education that they would not find anywhere else. Once educated, the members moved into society as teachers, even if only by examples of the benefits of education.

Do you see why Freemasonry became so popular and spread so quickly to all corners of the world? Do you see why dictators and those who sought to rule by oppression saw

Freemasonry as the enemy? The truth is that Freemasonry has always been the enemy of ignorance.

Freemasonry was an active Order on an actual mission, and it was winning that war against ignorance. We know that Freemasonry itself did not create the United States, but certainly, Freemasons had a hand in its creation. Certainly, the teachings of Freemasonry played a role in the formation of our government. We were the *New Atlantis*.

But during the 1700s, there was more happening within Freemasonry itself and the world. Simply put, Freemasonry won the war. Of course, ignorance was not, and is not, gone from the world, but tremendous and positive changes have been made. Yes, Freemasonry did play a leading role in that change. And when Freemasonry did win this war on organized ignorance, then came something else that we may fail to see or overlook.

There is something that we should think about. If you work very hard for a very long time on one goal, such as replacing darkness with light, and this long, hard work succeeds, what next? When you finally achieve your goals, what do you then do? Remember, Freemasonry was not a club; it was an active Order with a very real and serious purpose. Freemasonry was a place of education. It existed to give the world something that it did not have, something that was very much needed.

The work Freemasonry was doing was also outlawed in many areas. As a result, a tremendous emotional bond was created between the Masons and the work they were doing for all humanity. Bringing light, education, to those who needed it was the sole reason for the existence of Speculative Freemasonry. But what role would they play after they achieved what they had been trying to achieve for so very long? That's the question that they faced.

The creation of the United States can be seen as the crowning glory of the work of Freemasonry. Freedom of thought, expression, and education was woven into the fabric of the young country. When the United States was created, people living here were cut off politically from England. It was necessary for them to form a new government. They created a government based on individual, sovereign states organizing themselves under a central federal government. It was a bold and new concept for a government.

But just as the young country needed to create a workable government, Freemasonry needed to reorganize itself in the new country. The Freemasonry that existed in the thirteen colonies prior to the revolution existed under the Grand Lodges of England, Ireland, and Scotland. Provincial Grand Lodges had been created in the British colonies to supervise Freemasonry in this new land. But once independence for the United States had been achieved, these Provincial Grand Lodges dissolved themselves.

Just as it was necessary for the young United States to organize itself into a government, so was it necessary for Freemasonry to reorganize. There was talk in the early days that maybe Freemasonry in the United States should organize itself on the model of Freemasonry in Europe. Maybe they should have one Grand Lodge for the whole of the United States. There was even talk of George Washington becoming the first Grand Master of the Grand Lodge of the United States.

After further talk and thought by the Masons in this new land, they came up with a different idea. Since states' rights were such an important and unique concept of the young United States, maybe Freemasonry should follow the blueprint already created. Maybe Freemasonry in the United States should organize with one Grand Lodge in each state rather than one for the whole United States. The Masons seemed to like that idea and developed it a little further.

After some discussion, they settled on having one Grand Lodge per state, one language per Grand Lodge (English), and one ritual per state, which would develop into the ritual commonly known as the American Rite (York Rite) or the Preston-Webb ritual. In Masonry around the world, this was as unique as the government of the United States. But remember that *concept of one* that created so many problems in the Dark Ages? Since the war on ignorance was basically won, could they have forgotten the trouble of this concept?

I can't get into the minds of the early Freemasons in the United States. I don't know why they felt the need to develop this concept of one. I don't know why they felt the need for every lodge, every Grand Lodge, and every Mason to, at least, try to be alike. The simple fact is that we are not alike, and it is nonsense to think that we are or can be. We all have our own likes, dislikes, strengths, and weaknesses. That's normal. But it seems that the early Masons in the United States wanted all of Masonry in our young country to be a mirror image of the other.

So, we had two situations happening around the same time in Masonry around the world. In Europe, Freemasonry was trying to find its new role in the world since its former role as a warrior of enlightenment was no longer necessary. While in the young United States, Freemasonry was adopting the impossible policy of trying to make every lodge into a clone of the other. What would the future bring? And that all brings us to the present.

Today, Freemasonry, too many times, resembles a second-rate social club rather than a center of education. Our transformation from an active Order to a pseudo-club seems complete. Our meetings too often are limited to a meal downstairs, opening the lodge, reading the minutes, paying the bills, and then maybe a little discussion on members who are sick as well as upcoming barbecues or social events. That's it. In far too many cases, the lodge experience is void of any education at all. And still, we talk about how special and important we are to the world. Really? Maybe at one time.

When members became bored with what we offered, they began seeking entertainment elsewhere. They stopped attending meetings or left us. When our numbers dropped to the point that lodges began closing and others found it difficult to pay bills, many lodges began dropping standards as to who they would admit. It was a vicious cycle.

The lack of education as to who we are, combined with taking in anyone who simply paid the fees to join, seemed to be the death blow for Freemasonry. But then something odd began happening. The young Masons who joined us wanted and demanded the return of Freemasonry from many, many years ago. They wanted the education, the esoteric philosophy, and the action that once defined us. They wanted what we used to be — Freemasonry, the verb. But the bond, the glue that once held Freemasons together, was the war on ignorance that they were actively fighting. But wasn't that war won and now over? Maybe not.

Today, we're truly seeing an almost war within Freemasonry itself. We see some with the club mentality who have been around long enough that they have worked themselves into leadership positions. For too many, Freemasonry is a means for feeding their ego. They like the grand-sounding titles, the authority, and the respect. Many are fearful that they will have to give all of this up. It feels good to be the big shots.

And then, you have the young Masons. They are satisfied with nothing but the teachings they know are hidden in our symbols and philosophy. They know that rank and office mean responsibility, not empty power. They will accept nothing but true Freemasonry.

So, what will the future be and bring us? I believe we will end up with a bright future. Freemasonry is once again becoming a verb. But this time, it's fighting what it has become, what it has withered into. Freemasonry is fighting those lesser human qualities and philosophies within Freemasonry. It is fighting itself to save itself. I do not believe that it will be an easy fight. But I do see a bit of light at the end of the tunnel. There is true power within the teachings of Freemasonry. There is a power within our symbols. Little by little, Freemasonry is again winning another war. This one is against the ignorance that was in control of Freemasonry itself for too long.

I believe we will see in the following years amazing things and, in the end, a return to true and pure Freemasonry.

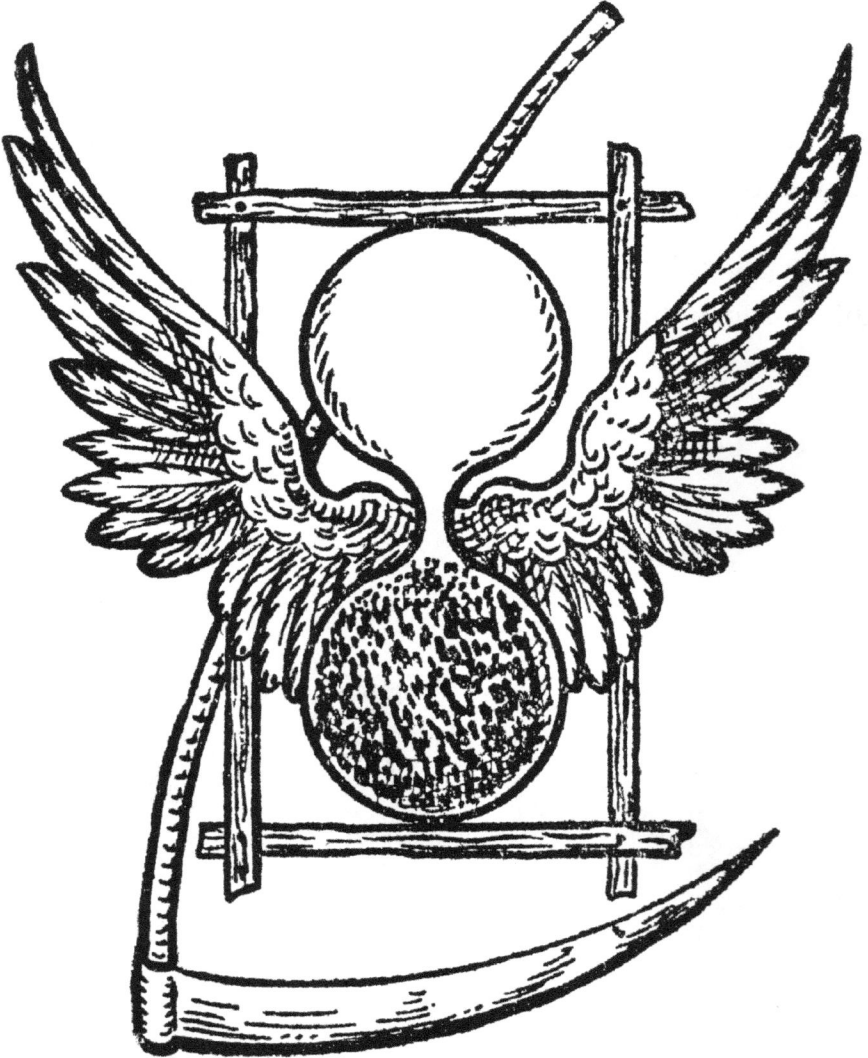

The Price of Kindness

As a kid, *Aesop's Fables* was one of my favorite books. I would read the short fables over and over again. I remember one titled: "The Farmer and the Snake." This fable told the story of a farmer walking through his fields in winter when he found a snake frozen on the ground. He felt sorry for the snake, picked it up, and placed it under his coat. The snake was quickly revived by the warmth, and, doing what they normally do, it bit the farmer. The farmer asked the snake, "Why did you bite me after I saved you?" The snake answered, "You knew that I was a snake when you picked me up." With his dying breath the farmer said, "I am rightly served for pitying a scoundrel."

In all honesty, I was always confused by this parable. What does it mean? On the surface, it seems to say that the farmer was unwise for trying to be kind to the snake. Was the snake actually a scoundrel for doing only what was instinct for him? Was the farmer reckless and was he being punished for his kindness? It all seems to call into question the battle between good and evil. What is *good* and what is *evil*? What should we do when faced with any degree of evil?

One thought is that in order to survive, we must destroy evil. But is that reasonable? If we believe in the balance of the universe, then evil must exist for there to be good. Darkness must exist for there to be Light. If we destroy one, how can we understand or appreciate the other? There is no balance in a scale with weight only on one side. So, if it is a fool's errand to try and destroy evil, how do we deal with it? How do we keep evil from overtaking us? Evil (even extreme evil) would seem to be only balanced by an equal degree of good — or maybe, wisdom.

The farmer was not limited to placing the snake under his coat in order to save it. He could have placed a blanket over the snake. He could have built a small fire near it. He could have understood the nature of the snake, protected himself, and still show kindness. God has given us a mind and the ability to reason. We need to use it. A good person is not limited to being a fool.

As Freemasons we are taught that our goal is self-improvement. We are given many moral lessons and guides to help us accomplish this quest. The problems in life and the number of possible difficult situations are countless. Not every problem always has a happy ending. The Lesson of Hiram is an example of doing the right thing at a terrible cost. But he seems to have had no option if he wanted to remain honorable. Unfortunately, doing what is right can sometimes be horribly difficult. We do it or we don't. Hiram could have given them what they wanted and possibly lived. But he would have lived out his days in shame of his failure. He would know that he was without honor.

We are not going to destroy evil, but not every battle with it needs to end badly. By using our minds, we can push aside evil and keep our integrity. We can show kindness to all and still keep evil at arm's length. If we know someone is unworthy, we can isolate and avoid them. We don't have to embrace them. There will be times when it is necessary to cut off an arm in order to save the body, but not always. In a lodge setting, if we know in our heart that someone needs to have more rough edges removed, then we do not give them positions or offices where the rough edges can do harm to anyone. We need to be responsible as well as kind. We must have the best interest of Freemasonry and our lodge at heart. It is not always a choice of only suspension or allowing someone to do whatever they want. It is very possible to be kind, strong, and still wise.

The point of a parable is not to give us clear answers but to make us think. I don't believe that the point of the parable of the farmer and the snake was to teach us to walk away from helping someone if they are perceived to be evil. The point is to teach us to always consider the consequences of our actions, and to discover the best way to protect ourselves, and still show kindness.

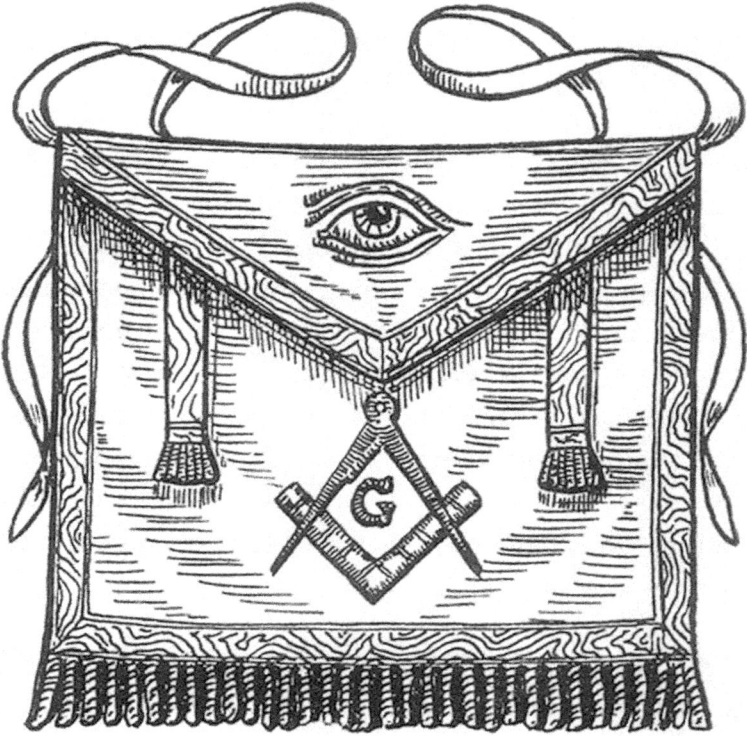

The Secrets of Freemasonry

I wanted to write a little on an aspect of Masonic education. I am a former editor of the *Journal of The Masonic Society*. I'm very proud of the publication. But the *Journal* itself is not the subject of this paper. I wanted to explain how a cover for one of the issues came into being and a most interesting comment that was made about it.

The cover for issue 41 is from original artwork by Bro. Ivan Ivanov. For each of the issues, Bro. John Bridegroom, our Art Director, found some outstanding piece of art and created a cover. I think the cover for issue 41 is one of the best covers that I have seen anywhere. The art was an esoteric/mystical piece entitled, *The Taro - A Path to Freemasonry* and consisted of three individual pieces of art: *The Emperor* (Hiram, king of Tire), *The High Priestess* (Soror Mistica), and *The Hierophant* (Solomon, King of Israel). I was very pleased with the final design of this cover.

So, as I normally did, I posted the cover in a few places online as promotion for the upcoming issue. I received one strong objection to the cover. It truly surprised me. The Brother said that he objected to the cover and would "skip" this issue of the magazine because it showed a woman on a Masonic publication. He said that he "should not have to tell us, but Masons are not to communicate Masonic secrets with women." I was, frankly, a bit confused by what he was saying and after a bit of thought, I simply sent him a few pieces of art from *Mackey's Encyclopedia*. They were all showing various women in this classic Masonic publication. I didn't bother with the countless other images of women in various classic and modern Masonic publications. I thought this would be enough.

The Brother answered me by sending back the very same comment, but this time in all caps, "MASONS ARE NOT TO COMMUNICATE MASONIC SECRETS WITH WOMEN." I refrained from sending him back a message saying that of all the things of which I have been accused, telling Masonic secrets to artwork on a magazine cover is not one of them.

I decided to ignore him.

But, in thinking about it, I realized that we are finding increased misinformation about what is and what is not allowed, or what qualifies as a "Masonic secret." I believe that when trying to deal with Masonic secrets, understanding why we have secrets is just as important as knowing the secrets themselves.

There must be some reason for something to be a secret. Safety and money are probably the two best reasons to keep a secret. If bad people are trying to hurt you and you're trying to hide away, then keeping your location a secret is important for obvious reasons. Likewise, if you own, say, a popular soft drink company then keeping your recipe out of the hands of the competition keeps you in business.

But, for what possible reason does Freemasonry today need to have secrets?

I believe that the reason is one of the less popular reasons for keeping a secret. When several people share a secret, even if it is a meaningless and unimportant secret, it creates a bond between them. They share something. It is this bond that holds together the brotherhood of Freemasonry.

In most parts of the world, Freemasonry is not outlawed. We are not under physical threat simply by being a Freemason. It is true that in some places where anti-masonry has gained a foothold, if someone is discovered to be a Freemason then their employment could be in jeopardy. In such areas, Grand Lodges seek to keep membership rosters private. But this is different than being stood up against the wall and shot for the crime of being a Freemason.

The secrets of Freemasonry are normally limited to modes of recognition and the obligations. Some jurisdictions consider the minutes of the lodge as secret. But since these minutes are written records most jurisdictions simply consider them as private and not to the level of a secret.

Sadly, some with obviously limited understanding of what is and what is not a secret, come up with silly ideas of what constitutes an actual violation of our obligations. The artwork that I mentioned on the magazine cover is just one example. I've heard some suggest that to even say hello or say anything at all to someone who belongs to a jurisdiction not recognized by you is a violation of our obligations.

It's just nonsense.

The problem comes when the nonsense is spoken by someone who has the authority to end your Masonic membership. Unfortunately, our lack of Masonic education spanning so many years has resulted in some with little to no understanding of Masonic practices gaining just about every possible office in Masonry. And, they have done so.

The answer is simple, or difficult, depending on your level of Masonic education. We need to teach, and teach, and then teach some more. I don't mean advanced philosophical or alchemical references in our work; I mean the basics. Too many Masons simply do not understand Freemasonry itself. They see it only as a place to get a hot meal, visit with friends, and listen to minutes. I cannot be more direct.

If someone is not entitled to sit in a tiled lodge of Masons, then you cannot share modes of recognition, obligations or anything that is reserved for a tiled lodge of Masons. It does not mean that you cannot speak with them about the general subject of Freemasonry. It does not mean that you cannot tell them the name of your lodge, where it is located or anything that is contained in any of the many commercially published Masonic books and encyclopedias. The vast amount of information concerning Freemasonry is completely open to the public. Any idea that this is not true is simply wrong.

I don't mean to suggest that we should argue with Masons who do not know something yet profess that they do. I also don't mean to defy those in authority who profess nonsense as if it were fact. I mean to avoid discussions with those sorts of Masons and gather with like-minded Brothers. Make sure that you know your law book, ritual, and customs. Make sure you are not actually the problem and then share and discuss this knowledge with those traveling your same path.

A growing number of Masons are discovering that by gathering at dinners outside of lodge, they are better able to explore Masonry than in the confines of lodges run by those with the club mentality. Now, of course, I mean to find out the rules of your Grand Lodge and follow all laws and customs required for such gatherings. But once you know that all is well — gather. I know of chartered lodges that have been formed out of these very sorts of dinners. Like-minded Masons gather, share Masonry, and then form lodges. It is natural that those who are on the same path travel better together.

There is no lack of loyalty or ungratefulness in leaving a lodge that is not a good fit for you. We all know that some lodges are in serious trouble. We know that the few members remaining want the lodges to be successful. But, sadly, most of these do not have members who are willing to grow or do the things necessary for their lodges to be successful. Don't fall into the "guilt trap" and remain in a failing club/lodge because "they need you." You can't truly help others until you help yourself. Get yourself in a true Masonic atmosphere and then you will be able to teach by example and thereby help all.

It may take a bit of time to get all of this to sink into the hard heads of those who believe that they know all, but it will eventually get there. Or Masonry will move on without them.

Freemasonry and the Courts

I'd like to talk a bit about a change taking place in Freemasonry. It's a change that has to do with new trends in the general practice of law, lawyers, and Freemasonry.

I'm writing this paper because we are in a time when acting responsibly may not always be easy. It's going to be very difficult to be a Masonic leader — and that means in the craft lodge or Grand Lodge. We will be required to act not only with integrity, but we will sometimes have to do unexpectedly hard things — possibly some very hard things.

Let's look at the situation.

I joined Masonry in the mid-1970s. One of my mentors was a Past Master and Treasurer of my lodge. He was active in the Scottish Rite Valley of New Orleans, having served in just about every position there. He ended up as the Treasurer of the Valley. He was by profession an attorney, and his office was just down the street from the old consistory building on Carondelet Street.

I visited him once or twice weekly to discuss Masonry and the Scottish Rite. In between our talks on Masonry, he would bring up other subjects. One thing that he often spoke about was the legal profession. He lamented changes that he saw taking place that in no way pleased him. He said that one concern was the cost of becoming an attorney. He said that unless a lucky law student was independently wealthy, he graduated from law school deeply in debt. Because he was in debt, he needed to find employment as soon as possible. The simple fact was that most new lawyers would not find work in high-paying law firms. And yet all new lawyers needed to start paying off their law school debts. The result was that they took whatever job they could get. He told me that too many of them became what he termed "ambulance chasers."

He considered being an attorney a very respectable and responsible profession, but he saw too many of the new ones "selling their souls," as he phrased it, for a paycheck. He would point to television commercials where he claimed these attorneys looked more like used car salesmen.

He made sense.

This wise brother told me that the law and the courts were sometimes being misused by a minority of hungry attorneys who were paying their bills by filing questionable lawsuits. Far too many were nonsense lawsuits that seemed to be only being filed to generate business for the attorneys.

As a result of his comments, I started paying attention to TV commercials. I saw ad after ad with smiling, healthy-looking people telling me that they received very large sums of money because they called the attorney in the ad after they had an automobile accident. Were they truly badly hurt, or were these ads suggesting that a fender bender could get me tons of money?

I would see large billboard ads all over the city and highways telling me to call some guy if I was in an auto accident, work accident, or pretty much if anything at all happened to me. I could get a huge settlement. Great sales techniques! I need money. Sounds pretty good and easy!

This trend of frivolous lawsuits also extends into other areas of life. Democracy is based on the concept of people with different political opinions working together for the common good of everyone. For democracy to work, more than one political opinion is necessary. They act as a form of checks and balances for each other.

Throughout history, those with different political opinions would fight hard for their opinion, their side. Still, in the end, they would compromise with those of different opinions to create policies that would appeal to as many people as possible. It is because it is normal to have different opinions and because it is recognized that sometimes we can become very rigid and emotional about our political opinions that discussions of politics or religion are forbidden in Masonic lodges. The lodge should be a place of peace and harmony. Hot-button subjects should be avoided.

But slowly, our political leaders have become far more rigid in interacting with those of different political opinions and parties. Where once the act of compromise was necessary to get something done in government, now we find unyielding "my way or the highway" attitudes are becoming the norm. In the US, this goes for both major political parties. When a politician wants to get something and needs more votes, a new tactic has been developed. Hit the other side with as many frivolous lawsuits as possible. Tie them up with lawsuits so that rather than getting anything done, they must spend that time in court dealing with legal matters that are mostly thrown out. It is a wily legal tactic, and it works. This is not to say that *all* court matters and charges are frivolous, but the ones that are problematic.

And what's so sad about these tactics is that every single one of us, regardless of our political party, are the ones who lose. The only winners seem to be those attorneys who write up, file nonsense lawsuits, and get large paychecks.

And then we come to Freemasonry.

The law and the courts have always been a part of Freemasonry. Buying property, acts of incorporation, and properly written bylaws are just a few areas where attorneys have been valuable and necessary to most lodges and Grand Lodges. And yes, there have been times when Masons or Masonic bodies have had to go to court to settle some valid legal matter.

Another area where Masonic attorneys are valuable is when Masonic trials are held for those who have violated any of the laws of Freemasonry. If attorneys are not part of the actual trials, they often function as advisors to ensure everything in the trial is done correctly and legally. At such times, competent attorneys have always been necessary.

But over the last few years, new developments have been taking place. Masons have filed lawsuits against their own lodges or Grand Lodges for a variety of reasons. Many of the lawsuits are so frivolous that they are quickly thrown out. But because Masonry has unique laws and we hold our members to higher standards than general society, sometimes courts, not understanding our rules and regulations, rule against lodges or Grand Lodges, causing a forced change in who and what we are. There is a tremendous danger when this happens.

I have spoken with a few attorneys lately about the growing incidents of lawsuits against Grand Lodges. This would be Masonic lawyers and lawyers who are not Masons. Both Masonic and non-Masonic lawyers agreed on one point. They said that all organizations must operate according to a basic standard as laid out in civil law. In other words, a Grand Lodge must follow its own rules and not do anything that would violate any civil or criminal law. They said that if a Grand Lodge operated outside of the civil law, they could be taken to court to force them to operate in a manner in accordance with the law. I was, frankly, stunned at hearing this. It was not what was being said that bothered me, but the fact that it was being said at all.

Let me put my thoughts in order and explain.

I once saw a TV court show that had an unusual case. Some guy was suing his ex-fiancée because she broke up with him. He wanted the relationship to continue, and she didn't. When you boiled everything down, he was suing her with the hopes of having the court force her to love him again or, at least, to remain in the relationship. How ridiculous! What was even more ridiculous was the fact that it was on TV. I guess they had an audience to watch that kind of nonsense.

But the point is that you can't force someone to feel something or be something they are not. No court in the world can force me to sprout wings and fly. I can't do it. There are limits to what can be accomplished by a court of law.

Now, stop and think a bit about how that applies to Freemasonry.

Someone once asked me if a regular Grand Lodge can ever become irregular. I told him yes, that if a regular Grand Lodge adopted policies that were contrary to the established Masonic rules and philosophy, then it would cease to be regular. A Grand Lodge itself is not Freemasonry. A Grand Lodge is Masonic and belongs to the Masonic family if it follows Freemasonry's teachings and embraces its philosophy. If it doesn't, then it is not Masonic, or it is no longer Masonic.

So, what does it mean to be Masonic?

Well, a Grand Lodge is Masonic if it follows the laws, customs, traditions, and philosophy of Masonry. Following civil law does not assure that something is Masonic. A social club can follow civil law. A social club is not Masonic, even if it perfectly follows every section of civil law. We expect *more* from Masons than does a social or civil club.

So, if someone believes that their Grand Lodge has treated them so unfairly that they can find no relief within the Masonic system, and fairness can *only* come by suing them in a profane court, then that's not a Masonic Grand Lodge. A Masonic Grand Lodge will not treat its members unfairly. It will follow the moral code as laid down in its laws. If a Grand Lodge cannot even meet the standards of a civil court, then it is not Masonic. It could be a poorly organized club, but it is not Freemasonry.

A Masonic Grand Lodge has rules and regulations in place for handling disputes between its members and between members and the Grand Lodge. But, if a Grand Lodge, or a small group within the Grand Lodge, perverts the Grand Lodge into, say, a dictatorship where the teaching and philosophy of Freemasonry are replaced with individuals seeking only to control the organization for themselves and without concern for the members, then this is not Freemasonry. If this happened to a Grand Lodge, then it would no longer be a regular Grand Lodge of Freemasonry, no matter what it calls itself. It's as simple as that.

If someone believes that this has happened in their Grand Lodge, then either they would be right or wrong.

Either the problem would be with the Grand Lodge or with them. Either the Grand Lodge would have ceased to act Masonic, or the individual would not be acting Masonic.

If someone believes that their Grand Lodge is no longer a Masonic Grand Lodge, then what should they do? Well, speaking only for myself, I know my time is valuable. I have no interest in belonging to a club that misrepresents itself as Freemasonry, much less a club that does not treat me well. I also know that if Freemasonry does not exist or no longer exists in a Grand Lodge, then no court in the world can turn an apple into an orange or a non-Masonic Grand Lodge into a Masonic one. It won't happen even if 100 lawsuits are filed, and the Grand Lodge loses each one. Even if the judge was a very knowledgeable Mason, he could not make a club into a Masonic body. He can only make sure that a club follows the civil law. Yes, a court can ensure that a Grand Lodge acts like a proper and legal club, but that is *not* Freemasonry.

If you are a faithful Mason and you know in your heart that the Grand Lodge to which you belong is no longer acting Masonic, and you feel that you cannot spend the time within Masonic channels to change what is wrong, then quit. Why would any sane person waste their time trying to sue a Grand Lodge to try and to force them into becoming Masonic? No non-Masonic court will ever be able to give you what you want. The most that a civil court can do is to make sure that a club follows the civil law. All you can do is try and work within the Masonic system in the hopes of bringing Masonry back to your Grand Lodge or quit. That's it.

But this is only if you are a true Mason.

What if you are not a true Mason, and the problem is really you? We must understand that lodges have failed to properly guard the West Gate for many years. We can give many reasons why this has happened, but it did happen. We are facing the problems caused by it.

Some of the unworthy who joined us have worked themselves into all positions, including the highest offices in Freemasonry. In the past, these unworthy Masons would live in their own world, like living in a bubble of their own making. They would have their titles, rank, and past offices of glory, but they would have nothing else. While they would project themselves as the most important thing in any room, the membership mostly dismissed them. Most members would recognize that these individuals were unworthy of the glory they attributed to themselves and were often of limited value to any aspect of Masonry. At least, unless a lodge felt it was beneficial to have a gold apron in a photograph. This, of course, is not reflective of all who have attained high office, but we can all point to those who fit this description.

Problems have come lately when some ego-driven past leaders act in ways that bring discredit to the whole of Freemasonry. In the past, when this happened, all Masons were held accountable for their actions. Lodge trials, suspensions by Grand Masters leading to trials in Grand Lodge, and even warnings by the Grand Lodge did take place.

Masons are expected to conduct themselves in a manner respectful of our teachings. When they don't, our rules and regulations have always provided a means to expel the unworthy. But when some of the unworthy are held accountable for their actions, a new trend is for them to file civil lawsuits claiming they were treated unfairly.

The courts are often unfamiliar with how Freemasonry operates, and even some defending Freemasonry can be unprepared or unfamiliar with having to deal with a court that is unfamiliar with Freemasonry. This can result in the unworthy sometimes winning and Freemasonry being forced to take back an unworthy individual. Our laws and rules are reduced to nothing. Our structure and moral foundation become compromised.

We claim to hold ourselves to higher standards, to be a moral organization, to have rules of conduct for our members, and yet we are at risk of the unworthy forcing us to reduce our standards and teachings. Ego, lust for power, glory, and status are sometimes being rewarded rather than having them purged from our numbers. The skilled and hungry attorney knows that by filing frivolous lawsuits in large numbers, he will probably get paid for each suit filed, and, who knows, he may win some of them. So, what do we do?

What do lodges and Grand Lodges do when the unworthy abuse both Masonry and the court system with the filing of unMasonic and frivolous lawsuits? What do we do when we follow our laws, hold the unworthy members accountable for their actions, and then see Freemasonry itself compromised when a profane court overturns what we've done because they did not understand who and what we are? Or still (and this is a bitter pill) what do we do if the filers of these suits win because of errors made by individuals who made technical mistakes due to their own lack of Masonic education? And even when they don't overturn our actions, they cost us money and tie us up in time by defending such nonsense and unMasonic lawsuits.

Freemasonry follows society, and we must recognize that the time has come when the insanity of legal abuse is reaching our doorsteps. The unworthy who take such actions against us must not be allowed to reduce us to their level or damage us by their actions.

The lodges that compose the Grand Lodge are also damaged when a Grand Lodge is damaged. When a Grand Lodge is prevented from doing the work it should be doing to defend ridiculous lawsuits from those who believe themselves above the laws of Freemasonry, then it is the lodges who suffer. When a Grand Lodge spends money to defend against these sorts of lawsuits, then we must understand that the money came directly from the lodges. It is the lodges that are being damaged and injured by these individuals.

The Grand Lodge is not some disconnected and far away body that exists separately from the lodges. The Grand Lodge *is* all the lodges under its jurisdiction. When the Grand Lodge is attacked, we must realize that it is an attack on all the individual lodges. The Grand Lodge officers *serve* the lodges of their jurisdiction. Any other belief or thought is part of the problem.

I know that many lodges are having difficult times. I know that getting through simple business meetings when hardly anyone shows up can be difficult. I also know that Grand Lodges are having difficult times. We are in a time of change, and no one should believe that we are not in the most challenging of times. What we do and how we conduct ourselves are, right now, extremely important.

Anyone who has gone through a Masonic initiation knows we are very special. We all know that we are so much more than a club. We all know that there are those who rise in rank but are unworthy. We also know those who lead us with honor and integrity. We know those on both sides. We can tell the difference. While it is never easy, it is time for us to act.

We need to pull together as Masons. We need to completely shun and disavow those who disgrace us. If any court would force us to take back someone unworthy by valid Masonic standards, then they must never again receive or hold offices or positions within Freemasonry. They must be ignored. They must be denied the one thing that ego demands of the power-hungry, and that is positions of authority and attention.

If a non-Masonic court forces Freemasonry to take back an unworthy individual, then this does not mean that our standards are gone, and this individual is correct in his manner of thinking or acting. It only means that we must be even more vigilant in our actions. We must be 100% Masonic. If such an individual steps one foot out of line again, he must be tried again. We cannot allow the fear of civil courts to force us to diminish our standards.

I'm not saying that it will be easy, but I am saying that it would be better that we close our doors than allow an unworthy Mason to force us to become less than what we are. If we are sued again for acting Masonic, then we must accept the ruling of the courts but never, ever cease to act Masonic — even if it means our own destruction. Reorganization is far better than existing as a quasi-Masonic body. No court can turn a club into a Masonic body. And likewise, no court can force a Masonic body to act unMasonic.

This will be our test of worthiness — a test of ego versus Freemasonry.

What we do will determine our true worth as Masons. In our teachings, the Grand Master Hiram Abif could have taken the easy way out. But he realized that if we are who we say we are, we must be willing to lose everything to keep who we are.

Do I Trust My Brother?

Someone once told me that people born in a city are far more suspicious than country folk. I grew up in a city, but on a military base (my father was an Army Colonel), so I was never really sure as to how my thinking was defined. But I do know that when I joined Freemasonry, my thinking on pretty much everything changed. Right out of the gate, I was put in the care of someone who I had no choice but to trust. I knew full well that, if he wanted to, he could make a tremendous fool out of me. But he didn't. I could tell by the tone of his voice and his actions that he was worthy of trust.

Following my initiation, I was told that everything that happened was designed to teach (among other things) a lesson of trust. I was told that we can, and should, trust our brothers because they *are* our brothers. That brought back a flood of memories of my grandfather who died when I was only 12. He was the reason that I wanted to become a Mason. One of the things that I remember of him was something that he said about Freemasonry and trust. He said that he would trust a Mason he did not know alone in his home with all his valuables. Was he foolish or did he know something that many miss?

My father was a WWII veteran. I remember him talking about trust and those who he served with in combat. He said that trust in those around you during that time was absolutely necessary. He said that in order to survive you had to be completely sure that the guy next to you had your back and was going to be there when needed. He said that when the fighting started, their training kicked in and everything that they did was a result of their training. He trusted them because he knew how they were trained and that they were worthy of trust. I thought a lot about what he said.

A friend of mine served in Vietnam. He told a different story. He said that towards the end of the conflict, when new troops came in, they were immediately sent to the front. None of the ones who had been around a while wanted to be anywhere near them. When I asked him why, he said that it was because they were dangerous. Towards the end of the conflict, basic training was minimal. The ones who had been around a while knew that the training of the new guys was so lacking that not only would they likely get themselves killed but all those around them. I found that as interesting as what my father had told me.

I've been a Mason now for going on 45 years. Just like I have changed in that time, so has Freemasonry changed. Some changes are for the good and some not so good. One of the "not so good" changes was our fear of declining membership some years back. Lodges were losing members and not getting new ones to replace the ones lost. We started taking in some who we may have rejected not long ago. We also started moving those who joined into leadership positions before they even knew the difference between a Landmark and a pancake breakfast. We traded education for fellowship. While we may not have seen it, we slowly started becoming something else — something very different than Freemasonry. To make it worse, it came on so slowly that most of us did not even notice the change.

Make no mistake, Freemasonry has serious problems. The lack of training of too many of our members has resulted in them viewing Freemasonry as only a group of friends. Too many do not understand who or what we are and allow fellowship combined with bad judgement to create seriously damaging situations. Our choice is to deal with the problems or watch our foundation crumble.

Recently, I read of a young girl who was attacked by an alligator. While being bitten, this child had the presence of mind to shove both of her thumbs into the alligator's nostrils. She remembered that this was what she was told to do if she was ever attacked. The alligator could not breathe, opened its mouth, and that allowed her to free herself so that she could get away. We need the same calm, presence of mind. We need the balance of both competent Masonic education and the backbone to reduce the unruly to order — to do what is needed. Weakness in either area can result in our failure.

As for trust, there may be another very simple reason as to why we have any trust at all in others. We trust because it feels good. Some scientists say that when we trust someone our brains release Oxytocin. Oxytocin is a hormone that promotes pleasurable feelings. We want to feel good, and we want to be around those who make us feel good. In other words, we have a basic need to trust others because it's good for us. But on the flip side, we also have something of a *sixth sense* concerning dishonesty that may be able to protect us from trusting the wrong people. Concordia University in Montreal published a study by researchers in their psychology department which found that children as young as fourteen months can differentiate between a credible person and a disingenuous one.[1] It's called balance. We want to trust others, but we seem to have an innate ability to know when trust is not deserved.

The reason my father trusted those around him in WWII was because he knew that they had received proper training. The reason my friend *did not* trust those around him in the later part of the Vietnam War was because he questioned their training. Far too often, even the Masters of lodges are completely unable to answer the most basic questions on the history, philosophy, laws, or customs of Freemasonry. It is very reasonable to question their "training." Is it any wonder that trust is lacking in Masonry? If we fail or are unable to trust our brothers, then we tear at the fabric of who we claim to be. We want to trust our brothers, we need to trust our brothers, and if we can't, it damages us at our core.

As with most everything, Freemasons have a choice. We can act, or we can sit back and do nothing. I believe that to do nothing seals a very bad fate for us. But I also believe that to do the wrong thing will bring equally undesirable results. I believe that the ability to know right from wrong comes from our training — our teachings. It's not enough that we say that we are Freemasons, we need to *be* Freemasons. We need to know who and what we are and live it. We are seriously sick, and we need to take some possibly bad tasting medicine. We need proper Masonic education. We need to make sure that all our members (especially those who lead us) understand our unique laws, customs, words, phrases, and philosophy. We need to be firm about this education. Without education or "training," we cannot trust our brothers. As difficult as it may seem, those who cannot or do not wish to learn, cannot lead us in any manner. We simply cannot trust an untrained Mason. The choice as to what we do about our current situation is ours. I hope that we are wise.

Notes:

1.
https://www.researchgate.net/publication/266137801_You_Seem_ Certain_but_You_Were_Wrong_Before_Developmental_Change_in _Preschoolers'_Relative_Trust_in_Accurate_versus_Confident_Spea kers

Why do we Memorize Ritual?

Have you ever knowingly done something that makes no sense at all? I'd like to look at something in Masonry that may not make a great deal of sense, yet most all new Masons in the United States do it. In fact, most lodge officers do this at every meeting. I'm talking about the memorization of Masonic ritual. Why do we memorize our ritual?

The simple truth is that I can't stand doing things that make no sense or are pointless. I don't mind doing something that is monotonous or boring if there is some usefulness to doing it. Another truth is that I am usually the one who gets myself into most of these pointless or undesirable situations. For example, I normally end up angry at myself when I ask someone how they are doing, rather than just saying "hello," and they start telling me all the unpleasant details of a recent, nasty break-up or some equally unnecessary information. All I really wanted to do was say "hello." It was my own fault for opening the door. The reasons why we do some things have always been a mystery and frustration to me.

One frustration that affects many Masons is the fact that many jurisdictions in the United States require their new Masons to memorize a Masonic catechism. Why? When I first joined Masonry, I wondered about that question. The answer I was given was that we memorize a catechism or ritual in order to advance to the next degree. That made as much sense to me as why I had to learn algebra in school. I was told that had to learn it in order to get to the next class. Yep, that was exactly why school was so frustrating for me. Telling me that I need to do something only so that I can get to do something else greatly irritates me and does not give me the information that I want. It only made Freemasonry seem pointless. The problem was that I knew Freemasonry was far from pointless.

After some time and research into the teachings and practices of Freemasonry, I learned that the way that we do things in the United States is not always the way that things are done elsewhere. In many parts of the world, the memorization of ritual or catechism is not required of new Masons. What is, however, required of them before they can advance to a higher degree is for them to write a paper on some element of what they have been taught and defend that paper in lodge. Master Masons will question the one presenting the paper (lecture). They will ask questions about various elements given to the lodge. The goal is to make sure that the one presenting his thoughts understands all that he is saying and not just repeating words with no meaning. That seems to be a far more educational task than just committing to memory a wide collection of odd sounding words and phrases with no expectation of understanding what any of it means.

So again, why do we require Masons to do memory work in order to advance? Well, maybe some things evolve for good or bad, and this may just be one of those bad cases. Maybe there was a very good reason for it that we may have forgotten. Maybe we have only part of the story.

I remember something that happened when I was a boy. I was in a toy store, and I saw a Lone Ranger figure sitting on his horse Silver. I wanted that figure so badly that I could taste it. My Mom told me that I could have it if I worked for it. I spent all weekend in my front and back yard pulling weeds, cutting grass, and doing everything that she told me to do. By Sunday evening, I had earned the money. We went the next day to go buy my prize. I worked hard for that figure, and the truth is that it meant more to me *after* I had worked for it. That seems to be the *lost* reason as to why we ask our new members to memorize ritual, and why so many outside the United States have them write papers. Both are to drive home the point that things that are freely given are usually worth what we paid for them. It is when we *do something* to accomplish an end that it is more meaningful for us. The entire structure of Freemasonry falls apart if everything is freely given for the asking. That's how we join a club. We ask to join the club, pay any fees, give them our name and address, and that's it. We become a member. That's not how Freemasonry was set up to operate.

But there is more to this puzzle of working for what you get. Why do some jurisdictions require new members to memorize and others to write papers? When I first thought about the two methods, I found greater value in new Masons writing papers. I joined a jurisdiction where memorization was expected. It was a system where I was given a series of words (a catechism) and asked to give them right back exactly as they were told to me. No one asked me if I understood any of it. All that I was asked to do was to repeat the words just as they were given. I saw little value in that. I had no idea why Masonry would ask this of new members. At first, I thought that it was to preserve the ritual. I thought it may not be written down anywhere. But I learned that was not correct. The Grand Lodge has an official ritual written down in Grand Lodge. So, it looked like I was back to square one.

I see value in someone receiving an initiation and then being required to demonstrate that it is understood by writing a paper on the subject. Over time, I began to also see value in the concept of memory work because of the instructor. Any time that a knowledgeable instructor is available, he can fill in the blanks and guide the student to a better understanding of the meaning of the work.

Both systems of the candidate "proving" himself made sense. An instructor helps the student understand the various events and symbols. He makes clear what happened and why something happened. He points out various paths for what can be very confusing and foreign to a new Mason. But something illusive bothered me. Was there more to this memory practice than I might see?

At times like this, I often put problems aside and let them rest a while. Pushing too hard on a problem that is resistant can sometimes result in forcing an incorrect answer.

Sometime later I was watching a documentary on the mind. They were talking about the value of doing memory work. Individuals were asked to write down their five favorite restaurants, five best memories, five of pretty much anything and everything. They were given a whole list of memories exercises to do daily. Every day they would do some mental gymnastics that required them to write various things down from memory. Numerous studies were cited showing sometimes amazing benefits for older individuals to stretch the legs of their minds. Exercise can certainly help the body, so why should it not also help the mind? I began thinking back to so many older Masons that I knew who were well into their 70's and 80's who had minds sharp as a tack, and each of them were very good at ritual.

Now, I certainly can't say that the cure-all for mental health is to study Masonic ritual, nor can I say that bad things can't happen to anyone. But I can say that it can't hurt to do memory exercises like studying ritual. It is a very good, calming thing to do. It can be meditative.

So, is mental health the reason early Masons in the United States began memorizing ritual? I doubt it. I believe that it had more to do with an appreciation of the old oral traditions. But I also know that education was a major part of all early Freemasonry — memorization augmented education. Over time it seems that the educational aspect faded away for the most part leaving only the memorization of ritual that mostly went unexplained. It's a shame. It's something that we need to fix.

I am personally convinced that memorization is a wonderful mental exercise that does have very good benefits for anyone. I also know that a Masonic lodge is a place of education. It is not just a place for physical and mental advancements. It is also a place for spiritual advancements. By understanding why we say and do particular things, and understanding the meaning of all we do, we grow as both Masons and human beings. Work for what you get. Study, learn, and then teach. Pass it on. That's what I believe we are all about.

The 24-Inch Gauge

I'd like to look at one of the symbolic working tools of Freemasonry. It's one that we learn about as Entered Apprentice Masons. To start with, I'd like to give you an excerpt from *The Louisiana Monitor*. If you're from another jurisdiction, this short section may vary slightly in the wording, but the meaning will be the same.

"The 24-inch gauge is an implement used by the Operative Masons to measure and layout their work; but we, as Free and Accepted Masons, or taught to use it for the more noble and glorious purpose of dividing our time. It being divided into 24 equal parts, is emblematic of the 24 hours of the day, which we are taught to divide into three equal parts; whereby are found eight hours for the service of God and a distressed, worthy brother, eight for our usual vocations, and eight for refreshment and sleep."[1]

So, let's stop for a minute and think about what's being said here. If we break it down, then we can see that the 24-inch gauge is a symbol for time management. We use it to remind us of how we can best spend our time during any day. But is this division of time workable today?

We are told that the 24-hour day should be divided with eight hours being devoted to the service of God or a distressed Mason, and then another eight hours for a job and then the final eight hours for sleep, or maybe sleep and eating. What about our family? Where do they fit in? What if we were required by economics to work more than eight hours a day? Is this a realistic division of our time?

I believe the lesson of the 24-inch gauge is a symbolic lesson. I don't believe that it was designed to be a hard and fast set of instructions. A symbol is of value to us because it can be used to teach us something that may not be obvious. I believe that the lesson being taught here is one that I have spoken of a number of times — balance.

I don't believe that we should serve God with a stopwatch in our hand. I can't imagine punching a time clock and ending God's work when our time is up. I don't believe that's what's meant here. The point is that we should balance our day with everything that's important to us as humans.

We must do something to be able to provide for ourselves and our family. We must be able to spend time with our family, to rest, to eat, to sleep, and to relax. We must do the work that we were put here by the Almighty to do and that includes helping others as well as ourselves. If we do any one of these things to the exclusion of all else, then we become out of balance.

Once we are out of balance, we're not able to properly do any of the tasks needed for a successful life. I believe that the lesson of the 24-inch gauge is to teach us to stop and look at the entire picture of our life.

We should spend our days doing what the Almighty intended, enjoying life, recognizing that we are only part of the whole. We should make sure that our life is spent in such a way that when we are gone, we will be remembered as someone who was worthy.

There is an old saying, "all work and no play makes Jack a dull boy." It's true. If all we do is try to earn money or do anything to excess, then we become out of balance. Our life will not be rounded and complete.

The lesson of the 24-inch gauge is not meant to teach us to punch a time clock and be rigid as to how we spend our time. It is teaching us that we ought to be fully rounded and do all the things that are necessary for a productive and valuable life.

Notes:
1. Huckaby, G.C., Compiler, *The Louisiana Monitor,* 1988, p. 31.

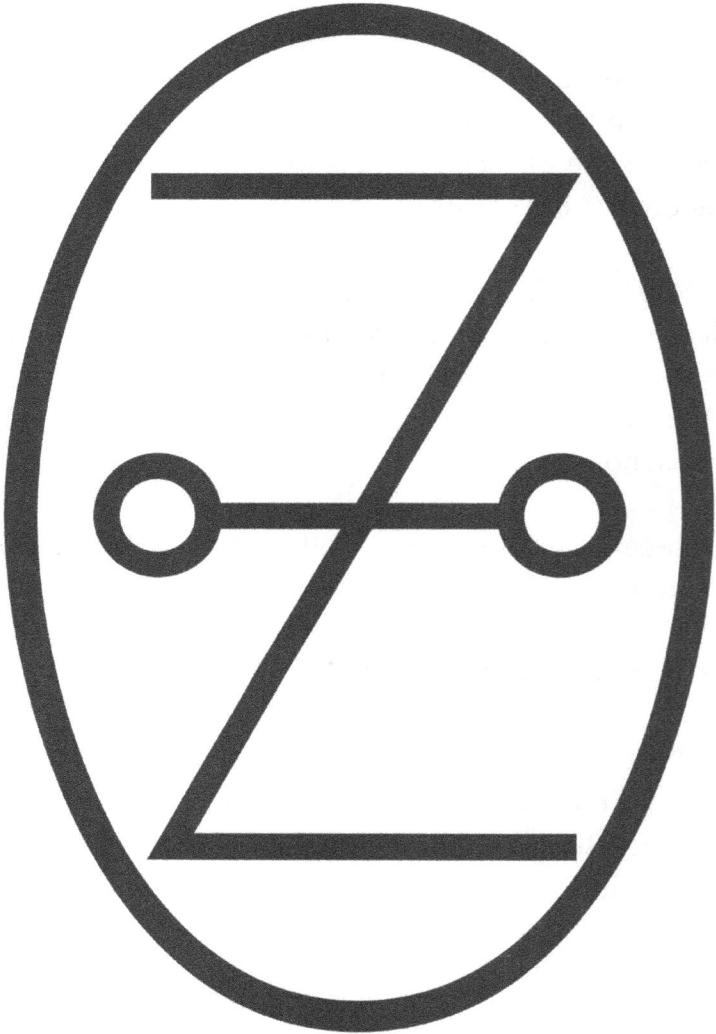

The Common Gavel

This paper looks at another of the symbolic working tools of Freemasonry — the Common Gavel, or in other words, self-improvement.

The first thing that I'd like to do is clarify which gavel we're talking about. The common gavel we will discuss in this paper is *not* the one used by the Worshipful Master and the two Wardens. These gavels are used mainly for instruction or information during meetings or degrees. Individual Masons or the entire lodge may be addressed with the gavel.

The common gavel that we will be discussing is a symbolic gavel that is used in Speculative Masonry by each Mason and for very specific reasons. Here is an excerpt from *The Louisiana Monitor*. If you're from another jurisdiction, this short section may vary slightly, but the meaning will be the same.

"The common gavel is an implement used by Operative Masons to break off the corners of rough stones, the better to fit them for the builder's use. But we, as Free and Accepted Masons, are taught to use it for the more noble and glorious purpose of divesting our hearts and consciousness of all the vices and superficialities of life; thereby fitting our minds as living stones for that spiritual building, that house not made with hands, eternal in the heavens."[1]

As with many of the symbols in Freemasonry, we have taken something with a common meaning and applied new meanings that may not be obvious to the casual observer.

We can think of our use of the common gavel as more of an action than an actual working tool. The common gavel can be seen as an act of self-improvement. The symbolic stone that is being worked on in Speculative Masonry is known as the rough ashlar. For an Operative Mason, the rough ashlar is a stone arriving directly from the quarry. At the quarry, they would quickly cut out a piece of rough stone and send it to the worksite. Then at the worksite, stone masons would smooth out the stones using their gavels. The stones would then be in a condition useful to be placed directly into whatever they were building.

In Speculative Masonry, we interpret the rough ashlar as an individual human being. He is of sound material but needs work. He's "rough around the edges," untrained, and untaught. He is said to be in darkness.

The common gavel is the act of smoothing out those rough edges or teaching him — bringing him to Light. The common gavel smooths out a rough ashlar for the Operative Mason and turns it into what is known as a *Perfect Ashlar,* or something useful for their work.

The goal of the lessons in Speculative Masonry is to take the sound, but rough and untrained human being, knock off all the rough edges and hopefully make him of such quality that he can live a more rewarding, spiritual life. He becomes a living Perfect Ashlar. He is useful to humanity.

If we think of an Operative Lodge, we can imagine rows of Operative Masons working on rough pieces of stone. They are all doing the same thing. They're trying to make their stones better than they were when they received them. They are doing the best possible work based on their skill.

In Speculative Freemasonry, we might think of the Operative Lodge as the entire Earth. The rough stone or ashlar is our life. Everyone is trying to do the same thing, make their life better. But not everyone will end up improving. Not everyone has the right tools or instruction. Not everyone has an interest in doing the work needed for self-improvement. But for those willing to do the work, the common gavel can be seen as that act that makes the good person better. This is a lifelong task. It's a task that ends only with the end of our physical lives.

The state of an ashlar at the close of anyone's physical life will depend on the work that they have done during their life. Of course, there are also rules regarding how we use our common gavels.

We might think of a large classroom or even an old Operative Lodge, with many people working near each other on their own personal rough stones. We can see the people around us doing their work, and we can see their progress. It's not, at all, considered cheating if we observe someone doing exceptional work and try to emulate them — to copy their technique in our work. It's also not considered cheating if someone sees what we are doing and tries to copy our work. This is considered working together and simply trying to lift each other up by example.

What is considered cheating is to directly involve ourselves in another's work. It's not allowed for you to chip away at another's stone any more than someone should be allowed to chip away at yours. We all do our own work.

There is a big difference between seeing another's work, recognizing the skill that's present in their work, and deciding for yourself that you want to do your work at that level of skill as opposed to doing the actual work for someone else. There is no personal advancement in having your work accomplished by someone else. For example, let's say that your friend's neighbor is ill, but needs some work done around his house. You going to your friend's house and helping out his neighbor secretly, allowing him to think your friend was the helper, (while kind) does not help your friend be a better person. We all must do our own work.

There is another aspect of self-improvement that I must cover. And it's not a very pleasant one. It has to do with envy. It's when we look at someone else's work and recognize the skill and quality of the work, but instead of trying to emulate that work in our own work, we become envious. We do nothing but stare in anger at the beautiful work of another. We allow the negative aspects of human nature to take control of us. We may feel envy, jealousy, and then bitterness and resentment. "Why can't *I* be doing work like *him*" Or, "Why should *they* be able to do what *I* can't do?" If ego controls us or guides our work, then destruction can follow. There will be no self-improvement at all.

Negative feelings not only prevent us from personal advancement, but they can place unproductive roadblocks for others. From an organizational standpoint, if our leaders are controlled by ego and lust for power or glory, then the only ones they will select as their lieutenants (the ones who will follow them) will be ones of clear lesser skill. Ego and envy will cause such leaders to hold back, deny advancement, or destroy the reputation of anyone who they believe could possibly outshine them. The quality of leadership will then diminish with each change that follows until the organization is of no value.

All of our leaders must be of the highest skill and moral quality. They must recognize that we all shine with our own level and variety of light. A leader *must not* be envious of the skill of another but rejoice when he finds great skill in the work of another. Great skill in a subordinate means the future success of the whole organization. The organization's long-term success should always be the goal of the true leader. Make no mistake, ego must never be allowed to take control. Ego can destroy all that we hold dear.

In any work towards self-improvement, we should recognize that generosity of spirit, kindness, and peace of mind are key to any successful life. But we must also recognize the need for unyielding determination to not allow the unworthy to gain access or remain in any sort of leadership position. A useful life must be of benefit to us and others. We must showcase the good work of others. We must recognize and hold up the good work of others as well as find ways to incorporate them into our own work. The work may be rewarding, but it will also be challenging at times.

When someone asks us for help, we must be generous but not do their work for them or demand that they make changes they don't desire. We must recognize that we all have our own paths. No one has the right to force an unwanted path on anyone else. And when our days are done, we must be ready to display our work for examination. Of course, the catch is that since we never know when that day will come, wasting time or putting off, until *later,* our work on personal advancements could be a serious mistake. Do your work now. Tomorrow may never come.

Notes:
1. Huckaby, G.C., Compiler, *The Louisiana Monitor,* 1988, p. 32.

The Domino Effect

Have you ever watched a table full of dominoes falling over? Sometimes they may be set in intricate patterns and other times simple straight lines. I've always found them fascinating. They are set up next to each other so that when one falls, it just barely touches the next one, but it causes it to also fall. This goes on and on for however many dominoes are set. They turn corners, go in straight lines, drop off cliffs, and create all kinds of pre-set, elaborate designs until finally all of them have fallen. When they are properly set, two things about this "domino effect" are clear: once the first one is tipped, unless something changes, they will all fall, and there is also no guarantee that nothing will change until they all actually do fall. At any time, you can remove just one domino from the line, and everything stops. I believe we can take something important from this that can apply to Masonry.

In many of our writings and explanations of Masonry, we inform the world that the design of Freemasonry is to make good men better. To be more useful is to be better. To be useful is to contribute to the advancement of the whole. But, the whole what? Are we part of something bigger or isolated entities seeking only personal goals?

The Domino Effect shows us that when individuals work together, beautiful things can happen. A single domino falling over means nothing to us, but many of them falling, one by one, in beautiful designs catches our attention and we do marvel at it. Working together, we can create more than going it on our own.

But we must never become complacent and believe that success is guaranteed nor become overwhelmed with feelings of doom. We all have free will and each one of us possesses far more individual power than we might imagine. At any time, anyone from a group can choose to step out of line and prevent either good, or bad, from happening. There is power in the group, but there is also power in the one.

So, if one individual has the power to step out of line and prevent something from happening, how can we know if his actions are helpful and not harmful? We can't know. If someone is skilled at causing trouble, they can hurt us. This is one of the reasons why we are supposed to take such great care in who we admit into Freemasonry. If we simply take any and all who apply, then the risk of the unworthy being in our group and causing us trouble dramatically grows. Once the unworthy are among us, it is only time before they become our leaders. With this, our whole fabric can unweave.

We were never told that being a Mason was worry (or trouble) free. We were, however, clearly told in our Masonic ritual lessons of the integrity that all Masons should possess. There are times when we must make difficult decisions. We must consider if we should, ourselves, step out of line to prevent everything from falling down in what we may recognize as an undesirable end. It calls for ample amounts of clear thinking, good judgement, and courage.

There are always two sides to every coin. There are times when working with the group helps create wonderful results. Other times, our decision to work with the group only makes us part of the problem and allows undesirable actions to become the result. Everything we do, or don't do, carries a result. Actions that we take can be positive or result in difficulties. Sitting back and doing nothing can also bring about negative results just as if we had taken the harmful actions ourselves. Should we step out of the line and cause everything to stop, or do we allow events to take their course?

Being a Mason can be difficult. If Freemasonry were only a club, then we should not expect much in the way of preparing us for challenging decisions. A club is often only a place to enjoy ourselves and find entertainment. But, if Freemasonry is much more than a club, and we are responsible, then we just might be able to find the guidance in our teachings that will let us know when to step out of line or when we must hold strong in that line. Many times, what we seek is right before us.

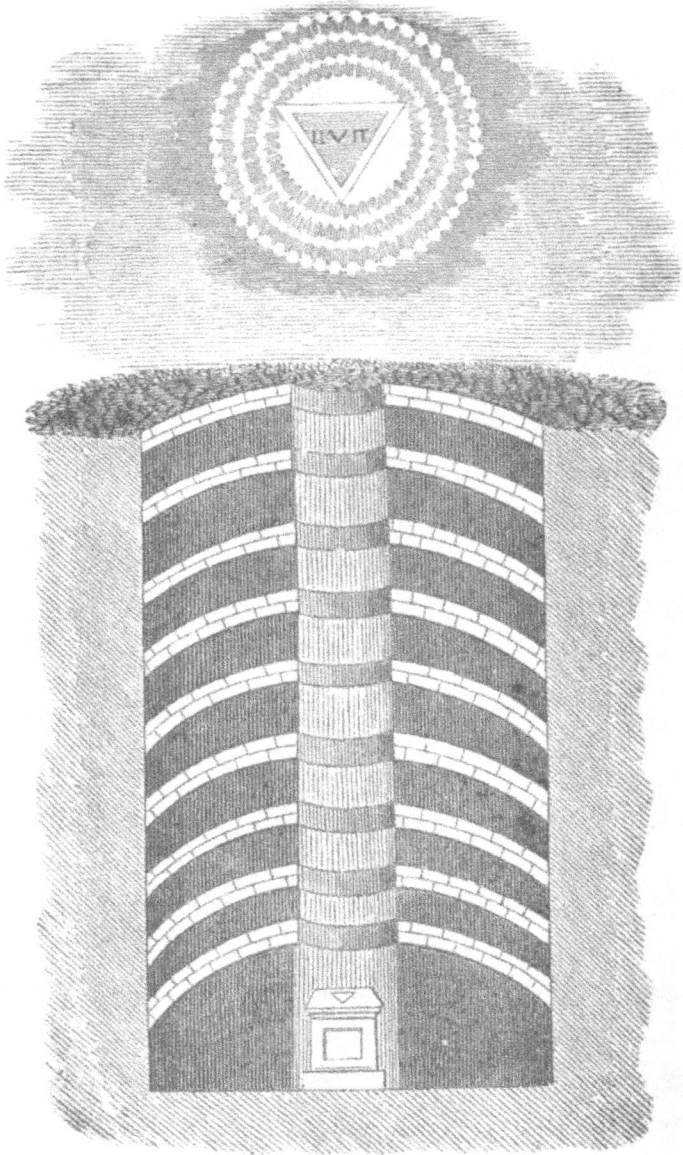

Rethinking the Ballot Box

Recently, I've had conversations with several Masons concerning problems we have today in Freemasonry. One Mason mentioned that we need to face the fact that many of today's problems began a good number of years ago with declining membership. He said that he felt that because of the concern for dwindling numbers, we did not pay close enough attention as to who joined us. He said that because we did not properly guard the West Gate, too many joined who should not have been allowed to join. They have now worked their way into all positions in all Masonic bodies. He felt that these individuals are causing us organizational problems. Another brother mentioned something along the same lines but added that we need to be quicker in rejecting candidates who we have questions about. We need to be stricter at the ballot box. Both brothers agreed that Freemasonry has a problem. They also agreed that we need to do something. I did a lot of thinking about what was said by them both.

Here's the problem. We know that something is wrong. We want to fix it. So, how do we do it? I believe that the first thing we need to do is to step back and look at the situation from a different angle. We must understand the nature of Freemasonry. It's not a civic society or social group. It is a moral philosophy designed to improve the quality of life and thinking of its members. If Freemasonry was designed for everyone, then we would not need investigation committees or ballot boxes. We would just take the checks and add the names of the new members. Even though some lodges almost do that very thing, we know it's wrong.

But there is more to this situation. If we reject someone, it is not necessarily a moral judgment. There are many reasons why someone should not be allowed to join Freemasonry that has nothing at all to do with their moral worth. If a man's wife objects to his joining Freemasonry, then he should not be admitted. Moral worth is not the issue. It does not matter how badly the lodge needs new members; Freemasonry is not about causing problems in its member's families. Likewise, if someone believes that Freemasonry is only a club, the investigation committee should correct him on this seriously incorrect belief. If someone with such a belief is not corrected, this is the way that he will view and treat Masonry. If he attends meetings and the lodge is hurting for members, he may soon become Worshipful Master. He will treat the lodge as he understands it. He may then obtain an office in Grand Lodge. He may even become Grand Master. It is certainly not at all impossible. He will still think of Freemasonry as another civic group and that is how he will not only define it but use his influence to shape it. The whole of Freemasonry will suffer.

So, what do we do?

The failure was on several levels. In too many cases our investigation committees almost rubberstamp candidates. They do little more than verify the candidate's name and address. Many jurisdictions now use a third party paid investigation service that will run a simple background check on the candidates to see if any red flags pop up. Too often we hear stories of how some candidate joined only to later learn that the investigation service missed something in his background. All blame is placed on the investigation service, but no blame on the investigation committee. Where were *they*? Why didn't *they* do a proper job of investigating the candidate? The investigation committees are not relieved of their responsibilities just because a Grand Lodge requires lodges to use paid investigation services.

One answer may be that the investigation committee was never trained. It is very possible that the reason that untrained investigation committees exist is because the Worshipful Masters did not know what was needed to train them — maybe because *they* are untrained. They advanced through the chairs quickly because they showed up. In fact, they may be the guys who joined thinking Freemasonry is only another club. The first line of defense for a lodge is the investigation committee. If they fail in their duty, or if there is a question in the minds of some members about *if* the committee is doing a proper job, do we just blackball the candidate?

I see problems on several fronts with blackballing any candidate that someone has only questions about or feelings that the investigation committee did not properly do their job. If we blackball a candidate because we are uncertain if our own investigation committee did a proper job, then the lodge has failed. It is a clear statement that not only do we feel that the candidate is unworthy, but the investigation committee is also unworthy. We seem to be saying that their evaluation of the candidate is not a valid one, and although they have approved this candidate, we know better than them. If this is the case, then why do we need an investigation committee at all? If we know that unworthy individuals have joined our ranks, if we know that we can't trust the judgement of our own investigation committees to be square or true, then what is the point of *anything* that we do? At some logical place we need to stop and rethink the entire situation.

I believe that in all of Freemasonry aspects of the lesson of Hiram play a larger role than we sometimes give him credit. In the Hiramic lesson, we learn of an unyielding and uncompromising integrity. Put yourself in his place. He made an unbelievably tough decision. At any point, he could have switched to the easy road and made his personal situation significantly simpler for himself. He could have said, "Oh, this is what you want? Okay, here you go." But, no, he refused their demands because he had integrity.

Sometimes being a Mason means that we must make the tough decisions and do things that are far from easy. If we have integrity and seek to do what is responsible, then we will try to find a way to do what we know to be right — even if it is terribly difficult. Step back for a moment. We know many have already joined Freemasonry who, maybe, should never have joined. This does not necessarily mean that they are bad or immoral people. It just means that either Freemasonry was not properly explained to them, or the investigation committee did not do their job due to carelessness or concern over dwindling members. Regardless of how they accomplished it, they did join us. You can't just throw them out. But it does present problems. We must act responsibly. We must always, *always* hold everyone accountable for their actions. We must put the best interests of the lodge and Masonry first. I don't mean selectively pick and choose who should be held accountable, I mean everyone should be held accountable by the same standard.

Some time back, I remember a lodge that had a truly awful Worshipful Master. He was not only unable to do any of the ritual work. He was unorganized, sloppy looking, often missed lodge meetings, arrived late when he did, and was generally incompetent. But do you know what? He was a nice guy. After his year was over, a Past Master of the lodge was talking with me about the problems in the lodge. I mentioned the situation with this Master. I told him that it was unfair to the brother as well as to the lodge to have elected him as Master. The brother told me that he disagreed because he felt that *everyone* deserves the chance to be Worshipful Master. I thought a good bit about that opinion and realized that this is the club mentality. If we are a club, and nothing that we do really matters, then yes, anyone can be Master and everyone who joins and shows up should be given this position — especially if the lodge has trouble filling the chairs. Are we a club or are we something much more? If we are something much more, exactly what are we?

If Masonry is a system of moral and philosophical education, then we must realize that this type of educational system requires specific training. I am neither a medical doctor nor a car mechanic. Sure, I can put Band-Aids on small injuries, but that's about it. Who in their right mind would come to me to diagnose a serious medical condition *or* a serious auto repair situation? If I am upfront and honest concerning my clear limitations, then anyone who would seek such advice from me would be displaying very poor judgement. I may be the nicest guy in the world, but if you are sick, then you need to see a doctor. If you know that your lodge is not doing well, then putting someone into office only because he is a nice guy, or maybe you feel loyal to him for showing up, makes *you* part of the problem.

If we acknowledge that Freemasonry is not a club, then we are forced to see it for what it is, a complex philosophical education system. This is what we are ... or, we are a club. Which is it? If we are a club, then we need no training, no expectations, and no accountability. We just eat, read minutes, and visit with our friends. If we recognize that we are something much more, and we care about Freemasonry, then we need to look at our present situation and rethink our priorities.

I don't believe that we should blackball candidates who have been approved by an investigation committee (except in extraordinary situations). If the candidate does not live up to what we believe a Mason should be, then we should never again appoint the members of his investigation committee to another such committee. If the new member does not live up to his expectations, then he should not serve in any office. If we don't have enough members to fill the chairs without unqualified members filling slots, then we need to close shop. Don't want to close shop? Then make sure that all who serve are qualified to serve. We are who we claim to be, or we are not.

How Much Fun is Too Much Fun in Masonry?

I've been thinking about something that I've written about in a few papers — balance. It's along the lines of the idea that a bowl of ice cream might be very good, but ten bowls will get you sick.

The concept of balance plays a large part in a successful Masonic experience. We truly should not discount it. And it doesn't matter if we are talking about a craft lodge, Scottish Rite body, York Rite body, or any organization in Masonry. If we go too far in any one direction, we fall out of balance and we will, before too long, find ourselves in trouble.

A while back I was contacted by someone who was concerned about a situation. He said that he wanted to talk with me about something that may or may not be appropriate in Masonry. He said that before joining Freemasonry, he loved comedy and had, during college, performed a little at a club as a stand-up comedian. He enjoyed making others laugh but worried that this was not fitting in a lodge.

I told him that I firmly believe that there is a time and a place for laughter and fun in a lodge, just like there is a time for seriousness. For example, it is very inappropriate for laughter or kidding around to take place during a degree or any aspect of ritual. But that hardly means that there is no place at all in Masonry for good humor or lighthearted activities. We just have to understand enough about Masonry to know when laughter is appropriate and when it is not.

It truly is all about balance. I knew a lodge that regularly held successful family nights where members of the lodge put on skits for all present. These skits were always well received. At such an event, a well-written comedy routine, even with the lodge as a subject, could be very entertaining. We just have to realize that problems can come when we display bad judgment by maybe taking a good thing a little too far in a lodge. The Bible is on our altar, no matter if it is opened or closed. We must remember that and keep things within the limits of good taste.

We must know when it is time to laugh and when it is time to be serious. If we just don't know what is crossing the line of acceptability, then we must seek out those who can help us learn what's needed. We don't want to end up being part of a problem in Freemasonry.

The lodge experience was never intended to be a joyless, unemotional, or dry experience. If the Worshipful

Master knows how to laugh and knows when it is appropriate to laugh, then the lodge experience can take on new levels of enjoyment.

I believe in the old saying, laughter is the best medicine. If we have good judgment, balance, and the ability to know what constitutes going too far then laughter in lodge can be a very important part of a successful lodge experience.

It is truly all about balance.

A Lodge's Worst Enemy

Not long ago I was at the District Lodge meeting. This was a meeting that was attended by Masons from several the area lodges. A few of us were talking about various problems the lodges were facing. One brother told a story about a member of his lodge who enjoyed arguing with anyone and everyone. Whenever the Worshipful Master made a ruling that he disagreed with, this Mason would stand up and loudly argue with the Master (or anyone else), and the arguments usually deteriorated into extremely unpleasant shouting matches. Little by little the lodge was attended by fewer members. The members simply had better things to do than go to a lodge and listen to arguments. This did not happen during just one year, but over a number of years with different Worshipful Masters. I listened to this story, and then asked why none of the Worshipful Masters did something about the problem. The answer that I received shocked me. I was told, "Well, what could they do?" Really? What could the

Worshipful Master do? Sometimes we are truly our own worst enemy.

The Worshipful Master presides over a lodge in much the same way as a presiding officer presides over any club or organization. But there are some major differences. For example, the Worshipful Master has far more authority in a lodge setting than a presiding officer has in a club. This is because our customs are based on traditions going back hundreds of years. The Worshipful Master is responsible for the lodge in all matters. If the lodge fails in any aspect, he takes the blame. As such, he is given unusual levels of authority to deal with problems in a lodge. It goes without saying that a Worshipful Master should be experienced, knowledgeable, and worthy of the responsibilities given him.

The Worshipful Master is never to be abusive, but he is responsible for maintaining order in a lodge. It is his responsibility to see that unruly members are "reduced to order." If someone in the lodge becomes loud, argumentative, or disrespectful during the meeting, it is the responsibility of the Worshipful Master to put an end to the disturbance. It may be as simple as dropping the gavel to end a discussion or as unfortunate as instructing the Senior Deacon to escort the brother out the lodge. He must do what is necessary to maintain order and harmony in the lodge.

But, when all this was explained, the brother came back with something rather surprising. He said, "No! You don't realize who we are talking about. No one can drop the gavel on *him*!" Turns out that the abusive troublemaker was also a "big shot." You know the type. He is the guy who if you upset him, he will deny you this or that "honor" or keep you out of all the "cool kid" bodies that you want to join. So, you grit your teeth and allow him to create upset in your lodge unchecked, right? No! Ignoring the problem only brings you right back to the first problem being discussed! These types of "big shots" are, regardless of their stations in the organization, a corruption of the teachings of Freemasonry. They are not an example for us. They are an embarrassment and displays of past failures. If we allow them to act up unchecked, then we share in the corruption of our teachings. I know that doing what is necessary may not be easy, but it's called being a responsible leader.

The role of the Worshipful Master is to guide and protect the lodge as well as instruct the members. If he is not prepared or qualified to do this, then the lodge has failed in electing him. If he does not properly protect, guide, and instruct, then he has failed in his duties. The Worshipful Master is to maintain peace and harmony in his lodge. It does not mean peace and harmony except for "big shots." It means peace and harmony. Period. If we are motivated in our actions by fear of not getting candy, then we have failed to learn what we should have learned beginning in the EA degree. In the end, we either do what is right, or we don't. We have integrity or not.

Reading the Minutes

I'd like to discuss a familiar activity in most U.S. lodges — reading the Minutes. Recently a brother told me of an encounter that he had with a Mason who told him that reading the Minutes was indeed an important part of the *total classic Masonic lodge experience*. This is a good example of how we can take something and twist it up just a little bit so that in time it can be completely misunderstood. Let me explain.

I'd like to look at the reading of the Minutes from a little different perspective. I don't want to look at the question (right now) of should it be done, but why it may have originally been done. I'd also like to look at the importance of the Minutes themselves.

So, let's start with the question of are the Minutes important? I guess the answer would be that it depends on if the Minutes are properly written or not. Accurately taken Minutes provide a record of the activity of the lodge for historical purposes. The Minutes should include which officers are present, the date and time that the lodge opened, and the time that it closed.

The Minutes do not need to be a word for word transcription of what was said during the meeting (except for special occasions), but they should include what happened. For example, if someone makes a motion to buy a new air-conditioning unit for the lodge, it's not important that the exact words of what was said be recorded. It is important however that the general intent be recorded.

If Brother Frank Jones makes a motion to buy a new air-conditioning unit, then that's what should be recorded. If Brother James Smith seconds the motion, that information should be recorded. If several brothers speak in favor of the motion, that information should also be recorded along with their names. If several speak against it, then that should be recorded. The outcome of the vote should be recorded.

The Minutes preserve what happened for the future. Let's say a few years down the line, the air-conditioning unit breaks. All the members will have to do is go back into the Minutes for all the information necessary regarding the details of the purchase and the discussion on the subject.

The Minutes should record everything that takes place in the lodge. Proper titles should always be used for all the members and a general, detailed account of the events taking place in the lodge should be recorded. The reading of the Minutes of the previous lodge meeting can be looked at as a form of checking up on the secretary to make sure that he properly performs his duty. Of course, it's only a responsible system of checks and balances and not any attempt at casting doubt on the ability or performance of the secretary. This would be the same idea as a yearly audit of the books. It's only something that is done because we are responsible. We check for errors, but we don't check because we assume that errors exist.

The reading of the Minutes is to make sure that something very important is done properly. And while it should not have to be said, the reading of the Minutes has no ritualistic or symbolic value. It does not advance the Masonic education of any of the members. It is only done to make sure that what is preserved in the archives of the lodge is accurate and complete. Of course, over time, reading the Minutes has become something that is always done after a lodge is opened. Because it is something that is "always done," we need to be careful that it does not become confused with ritual.

Also, if we are honest with ourselves, many of us tune out during the reading of the Minutes. If we were at the last meeting, we know what happened. Sure, every now and then someone may offer a correction for something, but generally we just sit there and listen to the Minutes … or check our email on our phone.

If the secretary keeps less than detailed Minutes, then it just means that we will have to endure the process for less time. No matter if we admit it or not, many of the members are a little relieved if the Minutes are kept short and not dragged out. Rarely does anyone think about any historical aspect of the Minutes or their importance to the future of the lodge. It's just something that must be done and endured. One interesting comment that I heard recently was in support of reading the Minutes in lodge. The Brother said that sitting there and listening to the Minutes is the "least that we can do for our lodge." What?? Does he mean that it is something like an elderly aunt telling us the old story she has told us 100 times before? We sit there and dutifully listen to her because she is family and she is, well … old. It has no deeper meaning or point. I disagree wholly with this sort of self-punishment. No aspect of Freemasonry should be some bitter pill that we force ourselves to take even though it doesn't help us, and we have no idea why we do it. Moral education is not the point or goal of reading the Minutes. Making sure that the Minutes are correct is the goal.

For any Masonic historian or researcher, old Minutes from a lodge are extremely important. From these Minutes we can learn what happened during any important time. The more detailed the Minutes the more information we can learn. Sure, if something happened a few years ago we can ask those members who were present and get a firsthand account that will likely give more information than is contained in the Minutes. But if are talking about something that happened 50, 100 or 150 years ago, then the Minutes of the lodge will likely be the only place that we can learn about the event. If the Minutes are sloppy or incomplete, then that is all we will have as a historical account of the meeting.

From a historical standpoint, a good secretary provides an extraordinarily important service to the lodge by keeping detailed Minutes. From a practical standpoint, a secretary who today keeps the Minutes as bare-bones and basic as possible, pleases most of the membership by not forcing them to endure a long reading of the Minutes.

Do you see the problem and the conflict?

Because most members today do not want to listen to a secretary drone on with a lengthy reading of detailed Minutes, the Minutes are kept short and basic. Only what is necessary is often recorded. It is doubtful that any thought at all is given to the historical aspect of the Minutes and the value they may or may not have 100 or 200 years from today.

If the practice of keeping Minutes is to provide a detailed historical account of what took place during a lodge meeting, and if the practice of reading the Minutes was originally designed to be a means of checking the accuracy of the Minutes, then we are today shooting ourselves in the foot. It's time that we stopped and give some serious consideration to what we're doing and why we are doing it. If we don't care and we just want to keep everything as it has been with no thought about why we're doing something, then we are contributing to our own failure.

The Minutes are vitally important to the lodge. It is not important that the Minutes be read so that everyone can listen to a recap of what took place at the last meeting, but it is very important to make sure that we have a proper historical record of the meeting.

More lodges today are realizing that the reading of the Minutes takes up time that could be spent on Masonic education. They also realize that if copies of the Minutes are printed and placed on the secretary's desk then it provides the same opportunity to verify the accuracy of the Minutes without taking up time during the meeting. But there are often objections to not reading the Minutes and only leaving printed copies to be reviewed. Why? Why are there objections?

Well, we often hear objections to doing away with the reading of the Minutes because we are creatures of habit. For as long as any of us have been Masons the Minutes have been read out. No other reason. No real thought is given to why the Minutes are read, only that they are read and have been read for a very long time — so we should continue to do it.

The benefit of printing up copies of the Minutes is not only with the time saved in reading out the Minutes, but it can afford the secretary the luxury of being more detailed with the Minutes without having to bore the members with a long replay of the last meeting.

We must understand that the goal of having Minutes is to provide as detailed as possible a record of each lodge meeting. It is not the act of reading the Minutes aloud that is important. It is making sure that the Minutes are accurate and complete. We must understand that when lodges began reading the Minutes, it was done at that time because they did not have computers or photocopy machines. They *had* to read the Minutes aloud if they wanted the members to have the opportunity to verify their accuracy. That's all that they could reasonably do. They did the best that they could do.

The secretary should make as detailed as possible a record of each lodge meeting. That is his job and what every responsible secretary will do. To prove that this job is properly done, the secretary provides those Minutes to the lodge for examination at the next meeting. That is his responsibility. It is the responsibility of the members to verify what he provides to make sure that all is correct. If either side fails at what they are supposed to do, then the lodge loses.

Lodges use electric lights because we have them. Lodges use air-conditioning units and heaters because we have them. We understand that 150 years ago lodges did not have either electric lights or air-conditioning units. We understand that they did the best that they could do with what they had. We use modern conveniences because we have them, and it's the smart thing to do.

150 years ago, lodge secretaries read out the Minutes because that was the only way that they could reasonably provide the information to the lodge without handwriting a whole stack of the Minutes. Today we can do far better. We can use our computers to print copies of the Minutes to be given to the members rather than wasting time on reading the Minutes out loud. We can use the time that is saved by doing what we should be doing — Masonic education. We are Masons, we teach moral improvement. The lesson of the

Beehive is not to teach us busy work. It is to keep doing what is most useful for the whole.

Of course, if, regardless of everything else, it remains our desire to have our meetings consist only of the secretary reading the abbreviated Minutes along with bills, and reports of who is sick or has died, then we can do that. If we want to bore and run off many of our new members by giving them pointless, empty work in place of Masonic education, I guess that is our right. Maybe we should give up our electric lights and central air units as well. It makes as much sense.

Understanding vs Misunderstanding

One of the advantages we have with face-to-face communication over any written communication is the ability to explain what words mean by simple facial and physical expressions. Many years ago, I worked with a very successful men's suit salesman. I was in college, and one summer, I was working in a clothing store. The salesman who outsold everyone had a unique manner of greeting customers. Anyone who walked into his area was greeted by him with very a loud, "What the hell do you want?" But I never saw anyone upset at him — at least, not for long. The salesman had a round, cherub face with a smile from ear to ear. His hand was always outstretched to shake the customer's hand, and you would hear a slight chuckle under his breath. Everyone could see that he was joking. His manner of greeting was so disarming, and his following actions were so inviting that the customers quickly saw him as a friend rather than just someone trying to sell a product. Without his unspoken physical communications, his words alone would have probably resulted in his being fired. His verbal and physical communication together, however, made him a very successful salesman. Communication is far more than just words.

It has been many years since I have worked with that very successful salesman, and communications (at least, written communications) have significantly changed since that time. The days of writing a letter to someone and mailing it at the post office have been replaced by e-mail and text messaging. It is so very easy to send someone a message with words today. I use text and e-mail more than the phone and far more than face-to-face meetings. The opportunity for misunderstanding is tremendous. And misunderstandings do happen when we text or e-mail. Unfortunately, along with misunderstandings often come hurt feelings, anger, and even argument. Just as e-mail and text can arrive far more quickly than a post office delivered letter, so do we arrive at hurt feelings and anger more quickly today.

The speed at which technology has advanced has given us something of a social whiplash. It sometimes feels as though we turned away for a moment to look outside the window, and when we look back, the whole world has changed. We are left trying to understand what has happened and how to handle the countless changes. We end up *frustrated*. We know that *we* did not make all these changes, so it must be the other guy who did it. The young people seem to have been born with computers in their hands. How did they learn so much so quickly about things that totally confuse us? All we did was turn around for a moment. We once knew what to do, how to do it, and were in charge. Now, we hardly know how to function in a world that has completely changed before our eyes. But we are still in charge! We oversee something that we don't understand or know how to manage. We see subordinates far more capable and proficient than us. It is *frustrating*! It hurts our ego. And there is the troublesome word — *ego*.

We are in a time of great change. Nothing can stop the change that's taking place. But how we react to change is up to us. We don't have to feel insecure because someone else knows things that we don't know. Insecurity brings about jealousy, distrust, anger, and conflict. We must understand that we all have our own strengths and weaknesses. We must understand that only by all of us working together, bringing together different skills and talents, do we all succeed. The young and older Masons need each other for different reasons. Only by all of us working together without thought of how we are perceived do we all grow as an organization or a society. The doctors, the musicians, the businessman, the carpenters — all of us have unique talents. We should look inward to improve ourselves and not envy the talents or skills of others.

The successful salesman communicated his message to customers in both words and actions. We should do the same and make completely sure that our brothers understand precisely what we mean. And like the salesman, our hand should always be outstretched to help those in need.

Scottish Rite Degrees and Honors

I have recently received two e-mails concerning aspects of the Scottish Rite that have caught my attention. Both e-mails had to do with a part of the Scottish Rite involving what is known as *honors*. The first question is: "What do you do if you see someone receiving a Scottish Rite honor that you know they don't deserve?" The second question is: "Further proof that there are only 29 actual degrees in the Scottish Rite is the fact that the KCCH *degree* and the Honorary 33rd are both given during honors weekend. How can you dispute this?" Now, the second question is not really a question but more of a continued debate by some that the 29 degrees given in a valley are the extent of the Scottish Rite degrees, but let's start with this question, or argument, first.

Sometimes, Masons develop strong attachments to whoever was their instructor in their early days of Masonry. I remember when a good brother told me something about the Scottish Rite that was simply incorrect. This brother took it as almost a personal insult or attack against the brother's memory when I corrected him. He told me that what he said was true because the brother he respected "never made a mistake." We must recognize that sometimes very dedicated instructors say things, and while they may be sincere in what they believe, they (like everyone) can make errors. Our job is not to tear down anyone or sully the reputation of any caring or deserving instructor. Our job is to simply present information that is factual and documented to be so. If we can't, we must identify it as an opinion.

Regarding how many degrees there are in the Ancient and Accepted Scottish Rite and the nature of the KCCH "investiture" (not a degree), I recommend *The Scottish Rite Ritual Monitor & Guide* by Arturo de Hoyos. This is one of the must-have books for anyone interested in the AASR. This book provides clear information on the Scottish Rite degrees.

As I am under the jurisdiction of the Supreme Council Southern Jurisdiction, USA, I will confine my comments to this body. The craft degrees of the Scottish Rite are *not* worked in any of the bodies controlled by the Supreme Council, Southern Jurisdiction. There are, however, eleven lodges under the jurisdiction of the Grand Lodge of Louisiana that do work in the Scottish Rite craft ritual. I belong to three of them and have served as the Worshipful Master of one. Regardless of what some might believe, lodges working in the Scottish Rite craft ritual do exist. It is a valid, beautiful, and very symbolic ritual. It is also very much a part of the Ancient and Accepted Scottish Rite system.

In the Southern Jurisdiction, a valley is the body that controls the degrees from the 4th to the 32nd. The Supreme Council administers the 33rd degree. This does *not* mean that the 33rd degree can only be conferred at the House of the Temple for Southern Jurisdiction. The Supreme Council can authorize the degree to be given in other areas. The point is that no valley authorizes or, on its own authority, confers the 33rd degree. The 33rd is always conferred under the authority of a Supreme Council. Other supreme councils have their own rules and regulations regarding which bodies control which degrees.

The KCCH is the Knight Commander Court of Honor investiture. It is given to selected 32nd degree Masons to acknowledge service to the Scottish Rite. It is not a degree but an honor investiture. The Grand Cross Court of Honor is the honor investiture given to selected 33rd degree Masons. This is also not a degree but an acknowledgment of service. Each has its own unique cap, and the investiture is part of the individual's record in the Supreme Council.

Now, confusion can come when you hear the terms "red caps" and "white caps." As I have mentioned, it is incorrect to say that the 33rd degree is honorary. No one is an "Honorary 33rd." The honorary aspect of a "white cap" is the office of Sovereign Grand Inspector General. A "white cap" does not hold the office of Sovereign Grand Inspector General (or SGIG or Active Member). In the Southern Jurisdiction, there are only 33 who hold this office. A "white cap" is an "Honorary Sovereign Grand Inspector General" or an "Honorary Inspector General." In other words, he has received the 33rd and final degree of the Ancient and Accepted Scottish Rite, but he does not hold the office of SGIG.

I believe that the root of the confusion may be in terms such as "honors weekend" or listing those who are to receive "red caps" and "white caps" together in lists. It does give the appearance that the two caps are different levels of the same honor. Regardless, the KCCH is an honor investiture for 32nd degree Masons, and the 33rd degree is the final degree of the AASR. Period.

Now, let's take a look at the second question.

The question of someone receiving either the KCCH or the 33rd degree and the belief that the one receiving it does not deserve the distinction is a particular problem. I want to spend a little time dealing with it.

I joined the Valley of New Orleans forty-five+ years ago. From time to time, you would hear comments about someone receiving something (a degree, investiture, or office) for which they are not felt to deserve. From what I can see, there are three categories into which these sorts of complaints can be placed. The first would be when someone receives either the KCCH or 33rd, and the belief is that the person who received it should not have received it. It may be because it is felt that another person should have received it (only a set number can be given out every two years). The second situation is more disturbing. It is when someone feels that another should not have received an honor because he feels that *he* should have received it. I see that as a very disturbing problem.

Another problem is the third situation. It is when others are not involved, but you find serious cause to question why a particular person is selected for any honor because you see that person as wholly unqualified and undeserving. The question becomes, did someone receive something only because of Masonic politics?

Let's look at the first situation where someone receives an honor, and it is felt that someone else is more deserving. There was something that I saw on television some time back involving the Grammy Music Awards (and this has happened twice). There was an individual who, after hearing the selection for an award, jumped up on stage and criticized the one who won the award, saying that someone else should have won it. In my opinion, this is a display of a total lack of class. Both the award winner and the one who did not win were clearly uncomfortable with the outburst. This public disturbance was embarrassing; however you look at it. The point is that if everything is equal and fair, and a limited number of awards or honors are to be given, then it is a subjective choice. It is a human choice. The ones selecting an award use their best faculties and make the best decision they can make as to who should get an award or who should maybe get it at another time. Bottom line: we must have some class! Everything is not about getting awards.

Let's say that honors are announced in your valley, and you believe someone deserving of some honor was not selected. There are things that you can do that deliver your message yet shows respect for everyone involved. I suggest that rather than tearing down someone who does receive an honor, go to the leadership in your valley. Mention this other person who you feel deserves something. Explain to the leadership what this other person has done and why you feel he is deserving of some honor. Maybe next time the honors are given, he will receive one. In all cases, and it does not matter if it is in a Scottish Rite Body, a lodge, or any other body, we are not about creating disturbances or showing anything but respect for the whole of Freemasonry. We are also not about having our focus on gathering awards. However, these are things that should be fundamental. If they are not, we might start wondering about the soundness of our own personal foundations. We all have disagreements with others from time to time. But you don't bring these disturbances to the lodge or any Masonic body. If you truly feel that someone is worthy and deserving of some distinction, then you praise that individual, but you do so without tearing down someone else or creating any disturbance.

In another situation, you may have someone who received a degree or honor, and you have a problem with the selection. But this time, you feel that *you* should have received it, not someone else. You feel that your work and service should have been acknowledged. You are jealous. There is no other word for it. Simply put, we don't have a place in Masonry for this sort of thinking. Our job is not to seek out honors, awards, or distinctions. Our job is to learn and then teach. That's it. Our job is to be of whatever service we can render.

I once heard someone say to one who received an award, "You deserve this distinction." I'm sure he meant well, but I disagree. I don't believe that anyone *deserves* any distinction, honor, or awards for anything we do in Freemasonry. Our *job* is to learn and then to teach. That is what we should be doing. Either we do it, or we don't. If we believe that doing work leads to receiving honors or distinctions, then receiving honors can become our motivation for doing things. Rather than doing something for the sake of doing it, we do it with the goal of being rewarded. This puts us out of touch with the philosophy of Freemasonry. I see this as a far more serious problem than simply preferring one person for an award over another. This situation places your wants or ego before everything else. With that, we need to wonder if we are qualified for anything.

So, if you feel you have been left out, overlooked, or even cheated out of some honor or office, think back to our teachings. Our job is to improve ourselves. That's what we should be doing. We are not improving ourselves if looking for titles or rewards is our end game. I suggest starting over and reviewing everything you have learned about Masonry from the very beginning. With an honest review of who we are, you should realize that seeking rewards for work is truly out of line with our teachings.

Now, the third aspect of this situation is if an individual receives some degree or investiture and, for some reason, there is a belief that he is wholly unworthy of this distinction. It is not a matter of preferring one person over another. It deals entirely with the individual receiving the distinction. If you believe such a thing, then you first need to determine if it is true. If you honestly feel that a person is unworthy, for whatever reason, then you must try and figure out why he would receive such a distinction — and if your feelings are correct. There are two situations where I can see where someone unworthy of a distinction receives something. One situation is that you never truly know what is inside another person's heart. You may find a situation where someone works like crazy and has all the outward appearances of someone truly dedicated. But then, when they receive some distinction, you never see them again. They disappear. They were not working for the sake of Masonry; they were working to receive some honor. When they achieved their goal, they stopped working. There was no need for them to work any longer. In such a case, this person would be unworthy. But how could anyone tell this before he received the honor? Yes, he was unworthy from the beginning, but he was able to disguise it. He was able to trick people. While leaders may regret giving someone such a distinction, there really is no disgrace on the part of giving such a person an honor. The leadership acted in good faith. They believed this person was worthy. Once it's done, it is done. The actual loss is with the person himself because he has failed himself. He is the real loser.

In the second situation, there is the suggestion that there is some deliberate attempt to give a known unworthy individual some distinction. But why would that be done? Well, the suggestion is that sometimes a political debt or payment is being satisfied with the honor. This takes the situation into a very unsavory area. If this is the case, then there are only a limited number of things that you can do. But we all must understand that everything we do is a matter of cause and effect. When we do something, there is a consequence for everything we do. If we are leaders, part of our job should be selecting people to be future leaders. Suppose we are elevating individuals to new positions of authority or rank in a valley or other Masonic body, and we knowingly take someone that we know is of a nature that is not in keeping with Masonic teachings. In that case, we are contributing to the downfall of our organization. If you are not in a leadership position and you see something like this taking place, there are only so many things that you can do. Again, I do not believe it is ever acceptable to cause a disturbance in any Masonic body. Freemasonry is a pure philosophy. If things are going on that are less than pure or unworthy of our teachings, then it doesn't solve the problems by acting in a way that is similar to what caused the problems. In such cases, you simply retire. You don't participate in this sort of activity. This is the best thing that can be done. If you join a lodge, and if the lodge turns out to be a problem, then there is nothing wrong with joining another lodge. The same is true if you discover something is going on in the valley that you know is unworthy of our teachings — move to another valley. This is a way to keep your personal Masonry pure and aligned with our teachings.

So, when we look at the situation of someone who we feel is unworthy of receiving a distinction or honor, it is a problematic situation in which to be placed. In the first place, we could be wrong. The person may be misunderstood. He could be very worthy but only unable to make his actual nature known to many. But if we are correct in our suspicions, what do we do? We must realize that we have Masonic trials because of the same reason we have erasers on pencils — sometimes, we make mistakes. We have taken in some who should never have been taken into our fold. We must recognize that there are cases when someone has been advanced for reasons that are not beneficial to the Scottish Rite or Masonry. This has happened. The problem is when a situation like this happens, and we keep it only to ourselves. We recognize that something wrong has occurred, are upset, and say to ourselves, "I don't want to be a part of this any longer." We then silently walk away. No one fully understands why we are not around any longer. I firmly believe that you should always speak to someone, at least one person. Let someone in charge know what is happening, why you feel you cannot attend meetings, or why you can't remain a member. It's essential to speak with someone so that they know what is disturbing you. Be open, honest, and straightforward. Either the problem will be corrected, or it won't. But, if more than one person feels as you do about this problem, the chances of it being corrected are better if all who feel this way speak out about it rather than remain silent and just walk. If members remain silent and just no longer show up, then no one knows why attendance or membership has dropped.

If you are a member of and understand anything about the Scottish Rite, you realize that you have a responsibility to it. It is our responsibility to safeguard the dignity and the teachings. I have never cared about the word "honors," as used in the Scottish Rite. For me, an honor is a little plaque that you hang on the wall and forget about. In my opinion, the Scottish Rite's use of the word "honors" should be replaced with "responsibilities." If we are offered a "responsibility" in the Scottish Rite, then there are certain things that we need to do. And one would be if we are put in an intolerable situation, we should not silently fade away. We should speak about the problem. If more people speak of a problem, they have a better chance of finding a solution. Of course, if nothing is done about the problem, you can move on to other things, but at least you have done your best to bring a situation and the problem to the right people's attention.

Freemasonry is of such a nature that we often get wrapped up in daily events and forget to look at the whole picture. In all cases, we must do what we truly feel is best for the Scottish Rite and Freemasonry as a whole. Anyone can make an error, but we must always act in good faith. We must do the very best that we can. We must also realize that sometimes, we must do hard things to remain faithful to our teachings. Sometimes, the simple truth is that members or leaders are unworthy. Sometimes, things are done that we know in our heart are wrong. If such a situation presents itself to us, we must consider everything and first put what is best for the whole of Masonry. While it is never good to create disturbances, sometimes the best thing is to walk away.

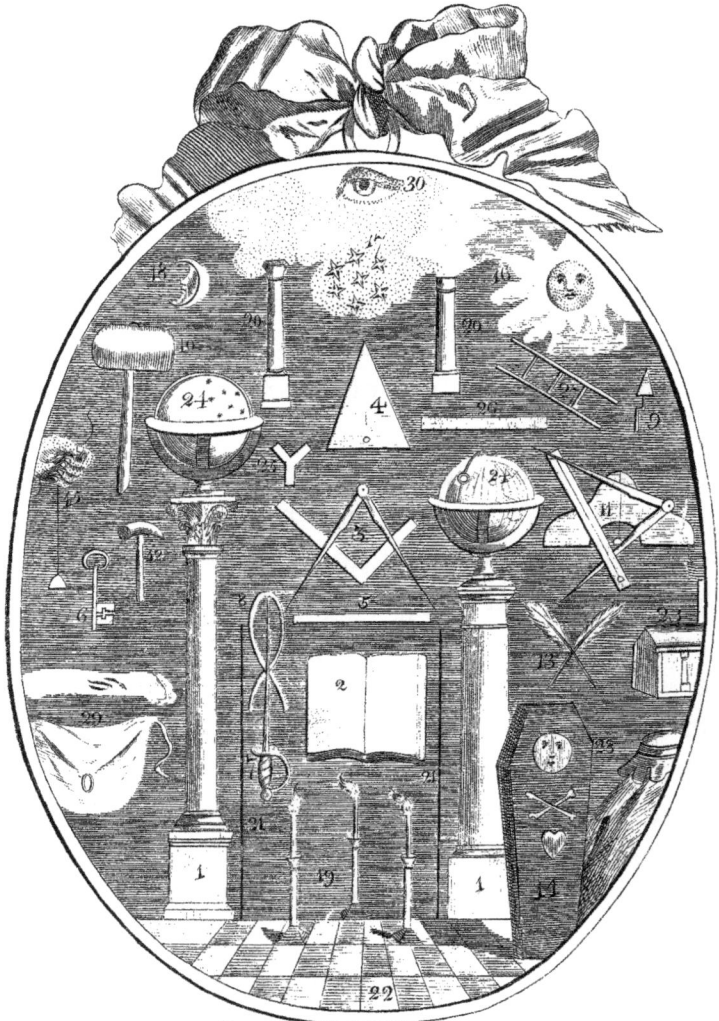

VIDE, AUDE, TACE.

5776.

Published according to Act of Parliament Aug.ᵗ 30.1776 by G.Nicoll.

Roberts Rules of Order – The Master's Friend or Enemy?

One of the most common problems faced by lodges is business meetings. But running a successful business meeting is also a challenge many clubs face. Sadly, one of the most common remedies offered for problematic business meetings and other issues in clubs and similar organizations is often incorrect for Freemasonry.

Let's look at the situation.

Roberts Rules of Order is the most popular and useful instruction guide for running any business meeting for organizations and clubs. The book gives clear instructions on the parliamentary procedure necessary for running any orderly business meeting for such groups. This book can be properly thought of as the most accepted antibiotic for any sick organization. Freemasonry, however, is the exception.

A disturbing problem develops when we see the classic *Roberts Rules of Order* advertised by Masonic booksellers as helpful to lodges. Freemasonry simply has different practices, and some of the guides and instructions in the classic *Roberts Rules of Order* do not apply to Freemasonry. The problem becomes greater when we see this book recommended by Grand Lodges. If you think of medicine, Freemasonry is allergic to the *Roberts Rules of Order* medication.

But don't misunderstand me; Masonic lodges do operate by use of parliamentary procedures. They are, however, specifically modified for Masonic use. I'd like to point out a situation where basic parliamentary procedure is needed and useful for lodges. After discussing how things should be done in a Masonic Lodge, we'll examine how the classic edition of *Roberts Rules of Order* can provide inaccurate information for a Masonic lodge.

Everyone who has attended more than a few lodge meetings knows that voting takes place in a lodge quite often. Someone makes a motion for something, and then someone seconds the motion. Maybe a little discussion is held on the question, and then a vote takes place. But sometimes, questions arise about the procedure and what is or is not proper. It is the questions, born out of a lack of knowledge of parliamentary procedure, that sometimes cause confusion.

Let's say that the lodge realizes that it needs new officer aprons. The aprons that they have are falling apart, and some of them have been lost. The Worshipful Master has already appointed a committee to investigate purchasing new aprons.

The committee makes its report, says that the lodge does need new aprons, and provides prices from several different Masonic supply houses.

The chairman of this committee makes a motion that the lodge purchase aprons for the three principal officers and names one of the supply houses as the place recommended where they should purchase the aprons. Someone in the lodge seconds the motion. The Master then calls for discussion. So far, all is going well.

Several Masons request permission to speak and talk about the condition of the aprons, past aprons bought by the lodge, and even how long it has been since they have bought new aprons — all good points. Then, a brother requests to speak and begins speaking on some upcoming event in another lodge. The Worshipful Master should immediately rule the discussion out of order. He does this because the only discussion that should be taking place at that time should deal with the motion being discussed. The lodge should be discussing whether they should purchase these aprons, as mentioned in the motion. Nothing else, at that time, should be discussed. Business should be handled one item at a time. If you mix things together or start something new before finishing what you started to deal with, you can expect confusion and disorder. Handle one thing at a time.

When no one else has anything to say about purchasing the aprons, the Master should call for a vote. Once the Master calls for a vote and the lodge has voted, the matter is settled. The outcome of the vote is what the lodge will do. But let's step back for a minute and go back to just before the Master called for a vote.

The only thing that can be discussed at that time is the motion concerning the aprons. But let's say that one brother has a problem with the motion because it limits the new aprons to just the three principal officers. He feels that aprons should be purchased for *all* the officers. In such a case, it's perfectly acceptable for him to request to speak and make a motion to *amend* the main motion. The main motion is to purchase officer aprons from a specific Masonic supply house for the three principal officers. The amended motion would change the main motion into purchasing officer aprons for all the lodge officers from a specific Masonic supply house.

Just like the main motion, an amended motion would require a second for it to be considered. The difference here is that once an amended motion has received a second, it needs to be dealt with *before* the main motion can be addressed. The reason is simple. If you deal with the main motion before the amended motion, then the only aprons authorized to be purchased will be for the three principal officers. The amended motion must come first, or it will not be considered. Therefore, anything that will change the nature of the main motion must be addressed before the main motion.

So, the Worshipful Master would call for any discussion on the amended motion. All would be allowed to voice their opinions or questions on the amended motion (and *only* the amended motion). When the discussion is concluded, the Worshipful Master will call for a vote on the amended motion. If the amended motion passes, this will change the main motion from buying aprons for the three principal offices to buying aprons for all the officers.

The Worshipful Master would then call for a vote on the amended main motion, and if it passed, it would mean all the officers would obtain new aprons.

But it is still not quite over.

Let's now go back to just before the vote on the amendment to the main motion. Let's say someone stands up and says, "Wait a second! I've had some bad experiences with this Masonic supply house." He says that he knows that another company costs a little bit more, but the service is better, and the quality of the products is superior. He is fine buying aprons for all the officers, but he believes they should buy from a different Masonic supply house than the one named in the main and amended motion. He makes a motion to amend the amendment to the motion. If this motion receives a second, it must be dealt with before the amended and the main motions. It becomes like building blocks. It can also get confusing if you don't keep things in order. Theoretically, this can go on forever.

To prevent "amendments forever," the Worshipful Master should always remember that motions should be as simple as possible. When a motion is being discussed, the Worshipful Master should be mindful that *all* aspects of the motion should be considered before a vote to avoid having to deal with amendments. It would be advisable for the

Worshipful Master to ask questions such as, "Is everyone happy with the style of the aprons or how many we should order?" or "Does everyone approve of this company?" The Master should bring up anything that might avoid an amendment to the motion before the discussion on the main motion ends. You must remember that any change or amendment to a motion (or a change to amend an amendment) needs to be dealt with before the main motion can be settled.

A successful Worshipful Master will understand the basic parliamentary procedure, Masonic rules and regulations, and where the two contradict each other. What must be understood clearly by every Worshipful Master is that in a Masonic lodge, Masonic rules and regulations must be followed regardless of what might be written or accepted as proper parliamentary procedure.

Let's talk about one of the dangers of the classic edition of *Roberts Rules of Order*. Let's say a lodge member wishes to make a motion on something. After hearing the motion, the Worshipful Master rules the motion out of order. In a lodge setting, that's it. It's over. Once the Master rules something out of order, there is nothing more that the lodge can do. The only option for the lodge members (if they feel that the Worshipful Master is incorrect in his ruling) is to go to the Grand Lodge. In a club, however, such is not the case.

The classic edition of *Roberts Rules of Order* clearly states that if the presiding officer rules something out of order, the membership is entitled to vote on the question. The membership can overrule the presiding officer by their vote and force the presiding officer to vote on a motion against his will. Any lodge that follows the classic edition of *Roberts Rules of Order* in such a case is going completely against the customs and laws of Freemasonry. In a lodge setting, the ruling of the Worshipful Master is final. It is because Freemasonry is not a club that the Worshipful Master is given authority not extended to the presiding officer of most clubs.

I was shocked when I first learned that the classic edition of *Roberts Rules of Order* was being sold by some Masonic supply houses and even recommended by some Grand Lodges. I knew that while many aspects of *Roberts Rules* were valuable to a lodge, enough of the book was seriously incorrect to make this book a danger to lodges.

It was then that I decided to revise the book into a Masonic edition that may be useful to Masonic lodges. The result was *Roberts Rules of Order: Masonic Edition*. This book was released in 1995 and has been widely accepted as a valuable Masonic tool for Worshipful Masters of lodges.

It is pointed out in the book that Freemasonry has customs and rules that differ from clubs, and each jurisdiction has its own rules and regulations that need to be followed by lodges under those jurisdictions. With the disclaimers and additions of landmarks, constitutions, and more, this book in the hands of the Worshipful Master, along with his Grand Lodge monitor and his jurisdiction's handbook of law, gives him the necessary tools for properly performing his office.

Accepting the office of Worshipful Master is something that no one should seek as a prerequisite to some other office in Grand Lodge or any appendant body. The office of the Worshipful Master of a lodge is one of the cornerstones of Freemasonry. The office should only be held by the most dedicated, qualified, and sincere Masons. Those seeking this office should be prepared to give it their all and always place the best interest of the lodge always first. A wise Worshipful Master will surround himself with good Masonic books of instruction as well as knowledgeable Masons.

The Masonic Rumor Mill

The rumor mill is a chronic problem going on today throughout Freemasonry. Years ago, I heard an old saying, "Men discuss, but women gossip." I also heard another that went, "Men sweat, but women glow." Well, guess what? Gossip is gossip, and sweat is sweat, no matter what we choose to call either of them or who is doing it.

When we talk about someone behind their back or when they are not around, that's gossip. That's pretty much it. So, what is the difference between gossip and speaking evil? Is one okay and the other not?

Gossip normally means revealing personal or private information about someone else. Let's say that you are told that a neighbor is cheating on his wife. You then take that information and tell everyone in the neighborhood about it. That's being a gossip. But is it speaking evil? Well, an argument can be made that if it is true, you have not lied about him. But you have taken information that will certainly hurt him and spread it around. Such a matter is private for the ones directly involved. So, is *speaking evil* limited to only lying? What about our claim of helping weak or fallen brothers? How is this helping him?

Spreading rumors does not help the one being gossiped about. It helps the one spreading the rumor. They feel that they are making themselves valuable by being the source of important information or, at least, interesting information. People love to be entertained, and they always love a good entertainer. Spreading rumors is no more than self-serving, cheap entertainment. Make no mistake; spreading rumors does not help the one being talked about.

And then, of course, what if the rumor you are spreading turns out *not* to be true? Can you claim that you can only be accused of lying if you *know* something is false? Can you claim that what you did was acceptable because you didn't know it was a lie? I don't buy that. If you pass on information about another and you have no idea if it is true or false, how can this possibly *not* be speaking evil?

One of the great excuses that I have heard about spreading rumors is that the one doing it did not "start" the rumor. They feel that they didn't lie or speak evil because they only passed on the rumor. Really? What sad nonsense.

When we talk about someone else and repeat something without even a slight investigation as to whether it is fact, then we own it. If it turns out to be false, we lied about someone else. That's it. All the excuses in the world do not change that fact.

Then there are also the ones who pass on some nasty bit of gossip but add the disclaimer that they don't know if it is true, but "this is what" they heard. "I didn't lie about him. I said very clearly that I didn't know if it was true!" Nonsense. Why would anyone pass on something that any reasonable person would know is harmful if there was even a suggestion that it was only a malicious lie? What kind of friend or *brother* would do that?

Character assassination is an effective weapon to destroy the reputation of someone. And this brings us to a most unpleasant subject. It deals with those deliberately spreading damaging information to discredit others. Some unworthy Masons use this practice to grab and hold onto bits of power or rank. They use the rumor mill as a reward or punishment. It is a horrible situation to think about, but it is a situation that, sadly, exists.

But, even if it is not your intention to destroy another's reputation, that can be the result of passing on rumors. This is not how Masons should act.

If someone is unworthy and has done things unworthy of Freemasonry, the remedy is a Masonic trial. To pass on harmful or damaging rumors about our brothers is itself unMasonic. If you have questions about the actions or motives of another Mason, ask them about it. Don't discuss it in little groups who don't know any more than you. Ask the one who is the subject of the rumor.

But is sharing information about someone improper if you serve on an investigation committee? You will need to talk about the one seeking to join. How do you fulfill your duties to the lodge if you can't speak about him? On an investigation committee, it is required that you attempt to determine the worthiness of a candidate. Once you reach an evaluation, you will need to pass your findings to the lodge. Is this gossip or acting unMasonic?

In all cases, we must apply reason, balance, and fairness. There is a difference between an investigation committee reporting to the lodge and spreading gossip to friends. If you discover damaging information about someone petitioning for Masonry while serving on such a committee, you are bound to take that information to the Worshipful Master. The information that you discover may well keep him out of Freemasonry. But you do not spread that information outside the lodge or the confines of your duty. What we do and why we do it is the key. There is a difference between doing your duty and knowingly hurting someone just to do it.

The same is true about elections to any office or any other time when an evaluation of someone is necessary for the betterment of the lodge or some other body. If someone is not felt to be qualified to hold an office for any sound reason, then it is just as bad for the lodge to put him in office as it would be to keep a well-qualified person out unfairly. The only way for a lodge to responsibly vote on someone is for lodge members to discuss their opinions of the abilities of individuals being considered for positions. This is done for the betterment of the lodge and not for the sake of gossip.

Our actions are to be fair, Masonic, and with all good intentions. If someone is unfit for office, then no mention of any election should be made to him. He should not have any reasonable reason to believe that he would be elected. If the individual is, say, a line officer, then it is reasonable for him to believe that he is being considered for and may receive a higher office. No one should automatically assume that they will always get an office, but it is reasonable to assume that it could happen. If voting members of the lodge (or other body) know that someone will not be elected for any reason, then they should let the individual know about it as much time before the election as possible. Allowing someone to believe he will be, or could be, elected and then blindsiding him on election night can only bring bad feelings and possible outbursts or disruptions in the lodge. It's just not Brotherly. It's just not fair. If we act only with the intention of hurting another or for idle gossip, then we are forgetting who we are and how we should act.

So, what do we do when we hear rumors spoken? What if others tell us of someone who is speaking evil of *us*, but we have no proof of it? We can't control the actions of others, but we have total control over our own actions. Let me give you an example.

In my jurisdiction, the ballot of a candidate is secret. One who reveals their ballot can be brought up on Masonic charges. This means that if one is unworthy, they can use the ballot to deny membership to someone for unMasonic reasons and be protected by the secrecy of the ballot. It is a powerful and effective weapon for the unworthy.

How do you keep the ballot box from being misused?

Simply put, you can't. Freemasonry assumes that our members are honorable and just. Our system presumes that if someone casts a negative vote on someone, it is because of an honest and just reason. Those who are unfit can abuse the system. It is the price we pay for belonging to a system that assumes the best of its members. The only way that we can stop such activity in any lodge or other Masonic body is when this is seen being done, to cease participating in that lodge or body. Let them dry up on the vine. I know that it can be difficult to do when a body can grant you titles, degrees, or other such trinkets. But situations like this show us what we are made of. If all true Masons cease supporting or participating in such bodies with unworthy members, then they will change or die.

No matter how you cut it, when you pass on empty rumors about another that has the potential to hurt them in any way, that's speaking evil. If you try to make the excuse that you didn't know that something obviously bad would hurt another, you are knowingly or unknowingly playing games. Masons don't do these kinds of things to other Masons or anyone.

But really, it's not only passing on rumors of what someone did or did not do that is harmful. It is also the unsolicited giving of others' negative and highly subjective opinions. "I know this guy doesn't care about the lodge or Masonry or this or that," or "I know this guy did *this* because of *this* reason." It's always something terrible. It's always that you have inside information that this other guy did or is doing something terrible. It is always your opinion, and, of course, you are completely right about this guy, even if you can't support what you claim with proof. The guy is just no good. If that's not speaking evil, I don't know what else it could possibly be.

Again, if someone has done something unMasonic and is unworthy to be a Mason, file charges against him; that is your duty. But if you act in a way that could destroy another's reputation only because you *think* that something is true, then *you* are the problem.

The old saying is true: if you have nothing good to say about someone else, then say nothing at all — sound advice.

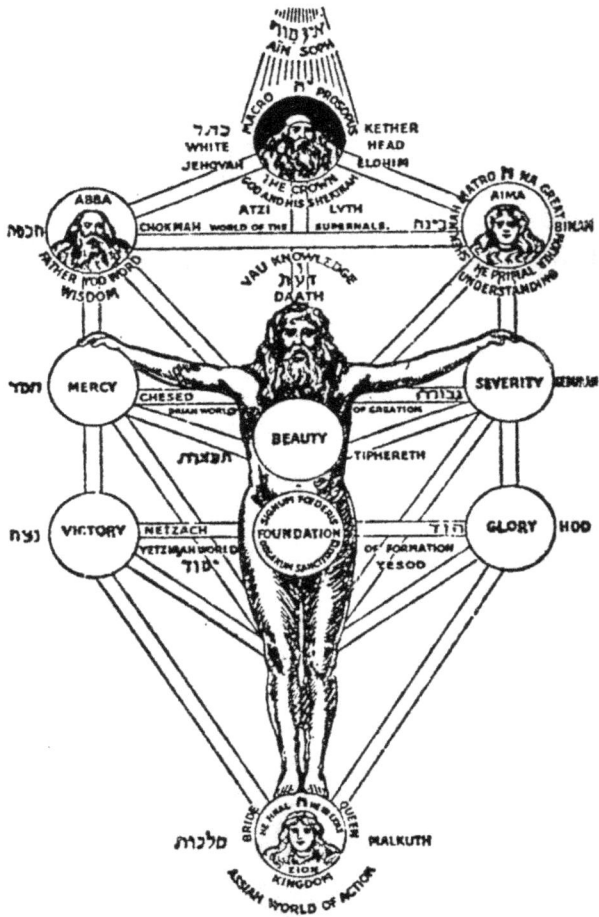

Why do we call it a "Blue Lodge"?

I'd like to look at an e-mail I received that addresses a common but sometimes difficult to explain aspect of Freemasonry. This question goes to the more abstract nature of our symbolic teachings and requires interpretation of our symbolism. In other words, there is not one answer, and it requires a bit of personal opinion based on a general understanding of symbolism. The question is: why do we call our craft lodges — *Blue Lodges?*

The most often answer given, at least that I have seen, is that the sky is blue. The old Operative lodges often met on hilltops, outside under the stars. So, is that the answer? They met outdoors, and the sky is blue, so we call our lodges *Blue Lodges.* That does give us an answer, but if we think about that answer, it also presents us with problems.

You see, the old Operatives were a labor organization. They worked during the day, and their lodges would meet for business after their work was completed. But, when would that be, at night or on the weekend? Some Masonic historians suggest that lodges would meet on those hilltops for their business meetings on Saturday afternoons. This would give them a blue sky above them. But are we sure about that? Are we sure that the old Operatives had a five-day workweek?

The Church controlled many aspects of medieval life, including work. Work on Sunday was not allowed. It was a day for rest and religion. This would seem to mean that there were no business meetings of lodges on Sundays. But what about Saturdays?

The usual eight hour a day, five days a week working schedule seems to be a modern invention. It seems far more logical that the old Operatives' work schedule was from sun up to sun down. They would work however many days of the week (Sundays excluded) that were necessary to complete their contracted job.

A nine to five workday does not seem practical for them as, for example, their days would be much shorter in the winter months. Daylight was necessary as they had no floodlights to see to do their work. They worked when the sun came up and until it went down. The sun was their clock.

So, if they held their business meetings on these hilltops at night, it would not be a blue sky. Maybe the answer is that they appreciated the blue sky of the day? Maybe. But maybe there is more to the answer.

Let's look at some other symbolic meanings regarding color. Blue is not only the color of the sky but of the clear sea as well. It often symbolizes heaven, wisdom, trust, loyalty, intelligence, confidence, faith, truth, and even the Word of God. The color blue has always been considered beneficial to the mind and body.

I've read of tests conducted with this color showing a slowing down of human metabolism, and just looking at the color can produce a calming effect. Dark Blue, or purple, is also considered a royal color and symbolizes purity and sincerity.

In advertising, blue is often used to promote products and services related to cleanliness or cleaning products. Blue is also for airliners, airports, and even air conditioning companies, suggesting an association with the sky, clean, cool air, or comfort.

We use blue for services or companies relating to the sea or water, such as cruise ships, or even some bottled water companies. Blue is also often used to suggest precision when promoting high-tech products. Blue is commonly viewed in modern society as a masculine color; hence, another reason that male Freemasonry may have adopted the color blue in its early days.

Light blue is often associated with health, healing, tranquility, understanding, and also softness. Dark blue often represents knowledge, power, integrity, and seriousness.

I believe that we would be hard-pressed to provide only one answer as to why Freemasonry associates blue to its lodges. But the most valuable symbols are those with multiple meanings or ways to speak to us. Any valuable symbol, by its nature, must be understood or able to be interpreted by more than one meaning.

In the early days, teaching by symbols was a means to provide information to students in an environment where some teachings were forbidden. A symbol might have a completely innocent interpretation to satisfy the authorities while still being able to provide deeper meanings to initiates. A symbol would provide both teachings and protection from those who did not desire such teachings to take place.

Such is the nature of a symbol and one of the reasons why Freemasonry finds such value in this form of ancient teachings. While we do not have the fear of authorities forbidding our teachings, we do have levels of understanding for our members. Some may wish only the superficial teachings of our Order, while others might wish to explore its deeper aspects. Our symbols can be explored with the goal of discovering their deeper meanings, or they also can be appreciated only from a superficial viewing or understanding of their total meaning. The choice is always ours.

By the way, I see blue as refreshing, pure, and inviting. That's my personal interpretation of why blue is used in "Blue Lodge." I may be dead wrong, but it feels good to me.

The Role of the Grand Master

Let's talk about an aspect of Freemasonry that is sometimes misunderstood — the role of a Grand Master. And while we are at it, let's also take a look at the Grand Lodge. I'd like to examine a few questions that are sometimes raised and problems that can develop from various misunderstandings.

Right at the beginning, it must be stated (once again) that Freemasonry is not a club. There may be aspects of our organization that give the appearance of the procedures and practices of a club, but to believe that we can run Freemasonry as we would run a social or community club is a serious error. We have ancient practices, customs, and regulations which are profoundly different from any club.

For example, the Worshipful Master is the presiding officer of a lodge. To believe that this office matches or is the equivalent of the presiding officer in a club is a dangerous mistake. The Worshipful Master of a lodge has authority far greater than that of the presiding officer of a club. See the chapter in this book on *Roberts Rules of Order* for more information on this subject.

Some who may not understand how Freemasonry is organized will argue parliamentary procedure and try to bully an inexperienced Worshipful Master (or even Grand Master) into changing his mind or reevaluating a proper (but maybe misunderstood) ruling. This only damages the foundation of our Order. We are not a club, and our rules and customs are in place for reasons that become clear only when our teachings are properly understood. It's one of the reasons why Masonic education is so vitally important. Once our fundamental nature and structure is altered due to ignorance of who and what we are, we may find it impossible to put the pieces back together.

The importance of studying your Grand Lodge Monitor along with your book of law and any and all Masonic books on symbolism or Masonic philosophy cannot be minimized. Successful lodges regularly use these books to guide their members' Masonic education. The Bible is not on our Altar to advance the Christian faith above all others but because the early Speculative Freemasons saw even more than religion in this Holy Book. While it is properly used as the Book of Faith for Christians, if religion is removed from the Bible, it is still one of the most morally insightful and philosophical books ever written. Many of the symbolic lessons in Freemasonry come from or are based on, symbolic lessons in the Bible. This book teaches everyone how to be good, decent human beings. The pure symbolic lessons contained in the Bible are of value to *all* humanity, even with its religious aspects set aside. Of course, for a Christian, it is a vital part of their religious life. But for any human on a path of moral enlightenment, the Bible is a most valuable tool for their journey. By studying any of these books, we give our members a proper foundation for understanding all our practices and the various offices we have in Freemasonry.

The office of Grand Master is based on the model of the Worshipful Master of a lodge. Whereas a lodge is composed of its members, who are individual Masons, a Grand Lodge is composed of its members, which are lodges. Lodges, composed of Masons, organize themselves into Grand Lodges. In the very early days of Speculative Freemasonry, lodges organizing into Grand Lodges made the task of determining who was and who was not regular far easier. For example, if you have two Grand Lodges, each with 50 to 100 lodges under their jurisdiction (and most Grand Lodges have more than that number), you will only have two Grand Lodges, or Masonic bodies, which look at each other to decide if they want relations. If they do, then all the lodges under each jurisdiction follow the ruling of their Grand Lodge. Without the Grand Lodges, up to 200 of the individual lodges would have to decide the matter of regularity by examining each of the other lodges. That's a *far* greater task. That's an enormous task. Can you imagine the work for the secretaries of the lodges?

Grand Lodges make decisions for all their lodges so that each lodge does not have to make so many decisions. It makes life simpler for individual lodges. So, when a Grand Lodge decides something, who is making the decision? Well, the voting delegates make the decisions. Who are the voting delegates? That depends on the Grand Lodge. In many jurisdictions, the three principal officers of the lodges vote along with the Grand Lodge officers and sometimes those who serve on committees or boards. Each Grand Lodge decides for itself who will vote.

The decisions made by a Grand Lodge fall into an area that confuses some Masons. In all cases, it is inexcusable for anyone who serves in any position requiring them to vote to be unfamiliar with their handbook of law or whatever the name of their Grand Lodge law book. Only by the officers knowing the laws can they properly make or uphold the laws.

I sometimes run into Masons who have outright anger at their Grand Lodge. They see it as a "them vs. us" situation. They view the Grand Lodge as some foreign, disconnected body that exists only to cause the lodge problems. It is an interesting and unfortunate situation. It also shows some confusion as to the actual nature and workings of a Grand Lodge. There seems to be an opinion that the Grand Lodge pushes its "will" through the Grand Lodge session, and whatever a handful of individuals in the Grand Lodge desire is the direction the Grand Lodge will go. That's, of course, possible if lodges don't care. But let's examine this situation.

Let's say that your Grand Lodge is not a very large one. Let's say that you have 75 lodges total in your jurisdiction. With Grand Lodge officers and various committees, they hold 50 votes. In fact, let's be generous and double that amount. Let's say that this Grand Lodge can be assured, with no question, 100 votes for anything they want. Those 75 lodges have three votes each, or 225 votes. That's more than twice the number of Grand Lodge votes with a generous count. Remember, each lodge has three voting delegates, so the more lodges you have, the more votes you have — times three.

The only possible way that a small group within the Grand Lodge can control anything is if no one attends Grand Lodge, doesn't vote, or pays no attention to the voting. It's all a numbers game. The side with the highest number wins. Of course, if you don't know what's going on, don't use your vote, or become truly knowledgeable in the events and situations, then *you* are the one who is to blame for any situation.

If we look at the office of Grand Master and don't correctly understand Freemasonry, we might well see a position that has far too much power from a club standpoint. I've heard it stated that a Grand Master does not have the authority to do this or that. I often hear such statements only backed up with opinions. Check your law book. Never listen to an opinion or accept a claim that something is in the law book. Have those claiming something is a law prove it, or do not accept it!

The Grand Lodge is made up of all the lodges under its jurisdiction. The lodges decide all laws and questions brought before it. The Grand Master is the presiding officer of the Grand Lodge. The problem is that the Grand Lodge meets only at fixed times, and problems can arise at any time requiring attention. The Grand Master is there to address problems or questions that come up during times when the Grand Lodge is not in session. His duties and authority are clearly spelled out in the law books.

Let's say that the Grand Master issues an edict (of course, this concerns Grand Lodges that provide for edicts in their law and regulations). An edict is a law or rule issued by a Grand Master during a time when the Grand Lodge is not in session. An edict is a law or rule that must be followed. During times when the Grand Lodge is not in session, the Grand Master has the full authority of the Grand Lodge. If the Grand Master says or rules something, then this is the same as a vote of the Grand Lodge. In other words, if the Grand Master says yes or no to something, then that is the law in that Grand Lodge.

The catch is that any edict, law, or decision the Grand Master makes is reviewed by the entire Grand Lodge when it comes into session. The Grand Lodge will approve or not approve any action by the Grand Master. If the Grand Master does something that the Grand Lodge does not like, then they can overrule him by vote.

But some exceptions and things need to be understood about proper procedure. In a lodge setting, if someone wants to make a motion for anything, the first hurdle is the Worshipful Master. Before anything else, the Worshipful Master must decide if the motion is in order. That means if it is a legal motion or will improperly affect some standing rule, law, or procedure of the lodge or Masonry.

If the Worshipful Master feels that a motion is out of order, he can stop it before it even receives a second. He can refuse to allow it to go to a vote. An example would be if someone stands up and makes a motion that affects the dues for the lodge during a meeting. The Worshipful Master would rule such a motion out of order as changing dues requires an established procedure in lodge by-laws and Grand Lodge law. Making such a motion during a lodge meeting without the whole membership notified normally goes against lodge by-laws or Grand Lodge rules.

In a lodge setting, a ruling that something is out of order by a Worshipful Master is final. The lodge cannot overrule him; the only recourse is to go to the Grand Lodge to argue why his action was not fair or correct.

If, however, the Worshipful Master allows a vote on a question, then he is bound to the vote. He cannot allow a vote and then set it aside by saying it is out of order.

Once the lodge votes, it is bound to the vote. If it turns out to be improper in any matter, it will take the Grand Lodge to overturn the vote of the lodge. The Worshipful Master has no authority to overturn a vote of the lodge.

Likewise, the Grand Master has no authority to overturn a vote of the Grand Lodge during a Grand Lodge session. If the Grand Master issues an edict during his year and the Grand Lodge votes to overturn that edict, the Grand Master has no authority to overrule the vote of the Grand Lodge. However, the Grand Master most certainly has the authority to rule out of order motions before the Grand Lodge, limit discussions, or not allow them at all. But like in a lodge setting, if a Grand Master does allow a vote on a question, then the vote of the Grand Lodge will be final during that session.

A Grand Master is given broad authority during his time in office to deal with problems of all sorts, answer questions, solve problems for lodges, and discipline Masons who violate laws. In each case, he is acting for the Grand Lodge, and each action will be reviewed by the Grand Lodge when it comes into session. It's part of the established checks and balances within Freemasonry.

So, what happens if a Grand Master abuses his authority? Yes, it can happen.

If that happens, there is very little that the rank-and-file Masons can do during that year. Thankfully, a Grand Lodge will usually police itself. If someone less than worthy misleads others to the point of being elected Grand Master and then begins acting in a way to bring discredit to the whole of Freemasonry, then Past Grand Masters will usually step in.

When his term is ended, not only will he see his actions overturned, but he will likely find himself without any further appointments in the Grand Lodge at all. He may be shunned and not become a welcomed part of the Past Grand Masters community. But great care must be taken so that this is a rare and not frequent situation. If unworthy, weak, or ineffective individuals reach this office in numbers, a disturbing trend can occur with extremely damaging ramifications.

If an unworthy individual reaches the level of Grand Master, then ego can be a guiding force with him. The position is a plum job for someone with an ego. Also, the position *after* one serves as Grand Master is a plum job for someone with ego. Some feel that a Past Grand Master is the power behind the throne and that they become the "King Makers."

In truth, with their ego in check and if they are well grounded, Past Grand Masters provide a valuable service to a Grand Lodge as experienced advisors. Their past service gives them insight into potential problems and solutions to problems that may be unseen or unknown to those with less experience in the Grand Lodge setting.

But, if a Past Grand Master is inclined or driven by ego, hunger for power, or any level of inability to perform his duties properly, then serious problems can develop if sides are taken and Past Grand Masters become split. The Past Grand Masters should serve as something of an anchor for the whole Grand Lodge. Their experience and dedication to service make them an asset to the whole Grand Lodge. But, if they become split, and worse yet if the reasons for their split have anything to do with questions of their lack of proper ability or ego, then the entire Grand Lodge can be negatively affected.

Grand Masters and Past Grand Masters are not above the law. In fact, I believe that because much has been given to them, and they have achieved the highest possible position in a Grand Lodge, they should be held to a higher standard. It's reasonable (but not desired) that a rank-and-file Mason may not know all the laws of Masonry. It is possible that they may not know certain things and make serious errors due to their ignorance of the laws or customs of Freemasonry. It's not an excuse, but it can be understandable — from a certain viewpoint.

But one who has served as a Grand Master of Masons in any jurisdiction is expected to know our fraternity's laws, rules, and customs. It is inexcusable that they would do anything to bring discredit to our fraternity. Any Grand Master, or Past Grand Master, who, through his actions, brings disgrace to any aspect of Freemasonry must be held wholly accountable for his actions — including expulsion.

Just as a rank-and-file, Mason can be held accountable if they turn a blind eye to another rank-and-file Mason who has committed a Masonic offense, so should any Past Grand Master be held accountable if they overlook another Past Grand Master known to have committed Masonic offenses.

Freemasonry must be defended and protected by all Masons, not individuals who have tarnished the reputation of Freemasonry by their unworthy actions — regardless of what office or position they have held. If Freemasonry means anything, we must require that all who lead are qualified and worthy. Violations of trust, honor, or duty must be dealt with in a manner fair and just to the whole of Freemasonry.

The Angry Mason

I'd like to look a bit at how Masons interact with each other — in both theory and practice. One of our early lessons is that a Mason should learn to subdue his passions. Basically, that means self-control. If you are in control of yourself, then you can do whatever it is that you are doing with a clear mind and to the best of your abilities. An old trick in competitive sports is to anger or upset your opponent. Maybe it would be a comment about the other guy's mother or some insult that would cause your opponent to lose control and do something reckless. This would give you the advantage. It is one of the reasons why the most successful in any sport are those who are in complete control of their bodies *and* emotions.

Over the last few years, I have seen disturbing displays by Masons showing a trend towards lack of self-control or an ignorance of how Masons should act or interact with each other. In previous papers, I've written on proper ways Masons should speak in lodge. Masons should use proper titles and show respect too all in lodge. I've also spoken quite a bit on the importance of Masonic education for all Masons — new and older. We need to understand who we are and what we are. But, over the last few years I have seen outbursts by Masons, both verbally and in print that have been frankly shocking. I've seen this in lodge and outside of lodge. I've even seen this in Grand Lodge settings. With my own eyes, I have seen a Mason being given the right to speak in Grand Lodge only to have him go into a tirade of screaming and yelling at the Grand Master and Grand Lodge, then rip off his credentials and throw them across the floor along with a handful of papers, storming off and out of the room. And this is not a singular event.

I have seen Masons not only yell and scream in lodge, but also use profanity in lodge, outside of lodge, towards other Masons, and write in the most insulting and insolent manner towards their brothers, lodges, and even Grand Lodges. I've seen this towards their own jurisdiction as well as sister jurisdictions.

I have seen just about every form of disturbing disrespect by Masons towards other Masons or Masonic bodies and then for these very Masons to act as if their actions are understandable and acceptable. Simply put, no, it is not acceptable.

I understand that we live in a world that follows trends and patterns within society. I understand that many today feel that it is perfectly acceptable to speak and write towards others however they like. They feel it is acceptable to be insulting, mean-spirited, crass, and pretty much however they choose to act towards others. But we are Freemasons. We hold our members to higher standards, and we are expected to control our passions. Doing things like "speaking evil" is what we profess *not* to do. It can even result in Masonic discipline. To allow Masons to speak evil without correction or consequences is as problematic as speaking evil ourselves. We claim to hold ourselves and each other accountable for our actions — or, at least, we should.

Our lodges are centers of enlightenment, not our local bar. We have altars in the center of our lodges upon which is the Holy Bible. It's there for a reason, it's not just a decoration. The Bible is there to guide us in our moral and spiritual improvement. Speaking evil is not taught in the Bible.

The goal of Freemasonry is self-improvement. If we are not able to control our actions or what we say or write, then we have failed before we even start.

Our Masonic experience will be what we make it, or what we allow it to be. If we want our Masonic experience to be reduced to a club experience, we can have that experience. But if we want more out of Freemasonry than just a second-rate club experience, then we must not only understand Freemasonry, but we must live it.

We should live and act according to our teachings. When we speak to our brothers, we must do so with respect. If we can't do that, then we should not speak to them. In Masonry, we are taught that it is better that we leave a lodge rather than allow disharmony in the lodge due to bad feelings with another brother. The whole point is that we do need to control ourselves. If we can't do that, then we need to not be around someone who can cause us to act unMasonic. At no time, however, are we to allow our spoken or written words to be anything but Masonic.

Make no mistake; it is never acceptable for anyone to cause conflicts in a lodge or to be disrespectful to our brothers or lodges. Failing to acknowledge or address such activity can be seen as condoning it. We all know when being upset turns into speaking evil. Those who believe that such activity should be overlooked have no understanding of Freemasonry.

If we see someone speaking evil (and that means telling stories about what some Mason did, cursing him, or in any way harming his reputation), we should warn the one doing this that it is unMasonic and caution him. If they continue, or if the offense is serious enough, we need to do the hard but necessary thing of filing Masonic charges on him. If we allow such unMasonic activity to slide, it only means that we are contributing to the failure of Freemasonry itself. It is not being hard or unfair; it is being a responsible Mason.

Write with Feeling and Meaning

I receive e-mails from time to time asking for tips or ideas for writing Masonic papers. The Brothers sending the e-mails sometime seem a bit uncertain as to what is normally expected from a paper. I'll put down some thoughts and my ideas of good and useful Masonic papers in today's world of Freemasonry.

Let me try to explain in a short story. When I was in high school, we had two school newspapers. One paper was the official school publication which was routinely judged in various competitions for high school publications. Truthfully, it rarely won anything. Also, truthfully, it was dry. Strict journalistic standards were followed by this newspaper. These standards were felt necessary to qualify them for the various contests. However … "strict journalistic standards" do not always mean an enjoyable reading experience.

The other newspaper was more of an underground newspaper, and while it was sanctioned and approved by the school, it was not considered the official paper. It tried to publish what the students wanted to read in a down to earth style of writing. The official newspaper was professionally printed (meaning also professionally typeset) on tabloid size glossy paper. It was a far more appealing publication to the eye. The underground paper was printed (meaning that it was typed out on a typewriter) on regular, letter size paper and run off on a mimeograph machine in the school office. The official paper published news of the school and the unofficial newspaper published news, cartoons, a "what's happening" section, and even a classified section. The official newspaper also had a far larger budget than the underground one. But as far as sales were concerned, it was no contest. The lowly underground newspaper consistently won by a landslide. I learned a lot by studying these two papers. One gave the students what they wanted, and the other simply tried to win awards.

The point in that story is that interesting reading material is what is going to be read and appreciated. Give the readers what they want. But it must be pointed out that the wants and desires of the readers can vary from publication to publication. If it is your goal to submit something to a particular publication, you need to learn a bit about their readership and publishing requirements. What is "interesting" is subjective and does change from place to place. There are also other considerations at play when a paper is accepted, or not accepted, for publication. Most all of the stories published in that underground high school newspaper would have been rejected by the official school publication no matter how interesting they were written. If someone wanted to write something for the official paper, they had to structure what they wrote according to the rules of the paper.

Before submitting something to a publication, read several issues first. Learn the style and type of papers that they are publishing. A popular publication is popular because what is being printed in the pages is liked by the readers of that publication. If you want your work published by them, then you must write something that is liked by their readership. If, however, a publication exists to fill a desired slot, accomplish a goal, or is dedicated to a particular subject, then you must submit papers that fill those needs.

A well written piece on the York Rite might well be published by any Masonic publication, but the first logical choice is to submit such a paper is a York Rite publication. Likewise, a scholarly Masonic publication might not be the best choice to send a light, feel good paper on an event in a craft lodge. Again, read the publication. Know the audience. One bit of advice is that all publications expect that if you write something, you are the one to support it. If you state that something is a fact, then the burden is on you to cite the source of your information. A quick way for your paper to be turned down is if you offer unsupported statements with the reader expected to prove or disprove what you have written.

Many smaller Masonic publications (but not all) are more lenient with styles and are simply looking for interesting papers to fill their pages. In such publications, the clever Masonic writer can shine. I suggest papers of general interest such as symbolic, esoteric, or new member oriented. Keep in mind that unless you are submitting a paper to a publication by your own jurisdiction, each jurisdiction has its own rules and customs. If you offer advice or say, "how something is done," you may be 100% correct for your jurisdiction, but 100% incorrect for the jurisdiction you are writing. Again, know who you are submitting to and their readers.

There is another point that I believe is very important and that is writing *for* your audience and not *at* them. It is the difference between using writing as a tool of communication to pass information on to others or as a tool to impress whoever reads what you write. One style is to help others, and the other to help you. It is possible to tailor what we write to accomplish a particular goal. If we know how to do this, we can be effective in accomplishing different goals with our message. If we simply put words on paper, then we might end up with just ... words on paper. Let me explain.

When I was in college, I signed up to take particular English class. My friends said that I would enjoy this class as the teacher was outstanding. They told me that he had three PhD's in English and truly knew how to teach a class. That information was good news. On the first day of class, I arrived a little early and watched everyone as they entered the classroom. I never met the English teacher before and knew nothing about him except that he was very good at what he did. I then saw what I believed to be an older student in blue jeans and a faded polo shirt walk in and up to the front of the class. He had longish hair and a beard. This was in the mid-1970s, but he looked more like a 1960s hippie. He put some papers down on the instructor's desk, smiled, and then said, "How y'all doing?" Then he introduced himself. This was our instructor — a hippie with three PhD's. He turned out to be one of the best instructors that I've ever had.

The hippie PhD is the one who taught me that language is a tool to be used in communications. It is to take ideas, thoughts, and opinions from one person and give them to another. Just like with any tool, we can use it for a particular goal, or we can misuse it. The teacher taught me that someone with outstanding language skills should not be confused with someone who has good judgement with language. For example, an attorney might have wonderful language skills, perfect for any court room. But, if he gives a talk to a class of 3rd graders and uses the same language that he uses in a court, then he has wasted everyone's time. He will be saying valid words, but he will not be understood. He will have failed to communicate because he spoke *at* them, but he did not consider them. We must know our audience and select our words to accommodate those listening to us or reading what we write.

And there is something else that I must mention. Once you start writing, you will find that some will say that everything you write is wonderful, and others will find fault with every word you put on paper. You *must* write in a way that pleases *you*. Either you will be successful with your style, or you won't. But you must write honestly and in a manner *you* like. You must objectively look at your work and decide for yourself if you believe it is of value. You can't let anything slide out of carelessness or be impossibly critical of what you write. If you are writing history, then you *must* properly cite what you write. You must check for typos and proof your paper. You must also realize that some typos will simply be invisible until they are in print. We are all human.

I often write something and then set it on the side for a few days unread. When I go back to it, I can see it with fresh eyes. I rewrite all the time. I am sometimes frustrated at allowing something to be published without some particular change. I also sometimes surprise myself and realize that something I wrote, and was initially lukewarm about, turned out a lot better than I realized. If it turns out that after a few days I don't like it at all, I toss it. But remember, being honest with yourself does not mean that you should only find fault with your work. It's okay to realize that something you did was good. Honesty works both ways.

Have fun with what you write. Write something you would enjoy reading. And please, don't edit your paper by looking for "bigger" words than the ones you used. The highly educated will know what you are doing, and others will only be put off by odd phrasings. But most of all, write. Do it and don't stop.

The Battle of New Orleans — *Filling in the Masonic Blanks*

A few years ago, Brother Pete Norman invited me to be the Anson Jones Lecturer for the Valley of Houston. It was quite an honor and privilege. When I arrived, Brother Pete drove me around the area on a tour of the various sites of interest. One of those sites was Holland Lodge No. 1. That was significant to me as a Louisiana Mason. Not only was John Henry Holland a Past Grand Master of the Grand Lodge of Louisiana (more times than anyone else), but he was a founder and first Worshipful Master of my Mother Lodge, Friends of Harmony No. 58 in New Orleans. Sadly, much of the colorful early history of Brother John Holland seems lost in time. So many of his actions and activities around the time of the founding of the Grand Lodge of Texas are unknown. Sadly, too many records were lost or destroyed.

Coincidentally, not too long ago, I visited Humble Cottage Lodge No. 19 in Opelousas, Louisiana. The secretary told me an interesting story about Humble Cottage Lodge and the founding of the Grand Lodge of Texas. He claimed that when Grand Master John Holland gave the warrant for founding the first lodge in Texas, a natural stop for the brother delivering the warrant would be Opelousas. He said that Opelousas was one of the usual routes from Louisiana to Texas. He also claimed that while the records of the lodge were destroyed long ago, it is likely that the brother would have visited Humble Cottage during his rest stop. I am still researching this account, but it does seem possible. And this is the problem with so much of early Louisiana Masonic history. So many of our early records were destroyed, and much of our early history is relegated to legend. This is what I will discuss in this paper — a bit of legend, lore, and logic. Some of it we know to be fact, but other aspects cannot be proven. The problem for historians is that we cannot discount logical rumors or unsubstantiated accounts of events because we know certain things did happen but cannot prove how or why they happened.

Let's start this investigation with look at a rather famous event in Louisiana history — the Battle of New Orleans. This battle is one of the most written about, talked about, and even sung about events in the history of Louisiana. We know that this was the final battle in the so-called War of 1812 between the United States and England. This war is sometimes known as the second battle of independence for the United States. We also know that this battle was about as decisive an American victory as possible and most likely propelled the commander of the American forces, Andrew Jackson, into the presidency of the United States. I grew up not far from where that battle took place. All through my childhood, I remember visiting the Chalmette Battlefield and seeing both the raised embankment behind which the American forces fought and a large open field where so many British marched to their deaths. Also, while growing up, I remember being puzzled by many of the books that I read on this battle. While the battle's outcome was the same in all the books, many of the specifics differed and were sometimes contradictory. Yet, these books were written by individuals who were considered competent historians. I began to realize that this battle had reached the level of legend. So many details of the battle identified as "facts" were exaggerations or outright made-up accounts of the events. I set a goal of trying to understand what happened during, before, and after the battle. I wanted to see if I could discover anything different or odd about what might have happened in such a historical and legendary battle.

Most accounts of the battle itself generally agree with the overall outcome. Maj. Gen. Andrew Jackson was given command of the American forces to defend New Orleans from a British attack believed to be impending. Jackson set up a defensive line about seven miles outside New Orleans at the Chalmette Plantation and waited for the British attack. Jackson's troops had fortified a natural levee alongside the Rodriguez Canal. From behind this levee, Jackson's troops would defend New Orleans. Maj. Gen. Edward Pakenham commanded the British forces. Pakenham's troops had landed a few miles below this location and marched to meet Jackson on the morning of January 8th, 1815.

On paper, Pakenham's plan seems to have been a sound one. The idea was for the British troops to advance in three columns. The middle column was the largest and was to march straight forward to engage the Americans. The two outside columns were to arc outwards to the left and right to go beyond the edges of the American lines and then work their way behind them. It was a classic pincer movement where the British hoped to attack the American forces from the front and rear. The British plan fell apart quickly when the British neared a large open area leading to the Americans. The Mississippi River was to the left of the British. The river took a sharp right bend at that location and came up almost to the British lines. This prevented the left column from arcing outwards. The left column, composed of the famed Sutherland Highlanders, the 93rd Regiment of Foot, was forced to march straight into the American cannons. The left column was decimated.

The right column did not fare much better. While the right column was able to arc outwards to the right, in doing so, they found themselves in the middle of a swamp. The fog was reported to be so thick that the British could hardly see their hands in front of them. They became turned around and lost. They soon began hearing gunfire to their left, which they assumed to be from the Americans. They decided to advance a little further and then turn to the left, which they hoped would bring them behind the American lines. Unfortunately for the right column, what they took for American gunfire was British gunfire. They were not behind the American lines when they came out of the swamp. They were between the

British and American lines and took fire from both sides. It was not a good day for the right column.

The main column of the British marched towards the American lines across an open field with no cover for them. The Americans had laid their long rifles on top of the reinforced embankment and began firing. For the Americans, it was basically target practice. The British, in their red uniforms, began falling. At the battle's end, the British's death toll was some 2,000, including General Pakenham and most of his command staff. The death toll for the Americans on that day was under a dozen. It is very easy to see how such a decisive win could have propelled all the Americans involved into superhero status. They were indeed the rock stars of the day. However, the death toll for the Americans significantly increased following the battle because of malaria contracted from being in insect-infested swamp water for days while they fortified the canal's levee. However, this higher American death toll was often discounted in most historical accounts as it did not portray the same romantic outcome as the death toll on the day of the battle.

Regardless of which account was read, I began to see a growing problem and one question for which I could not find an answer. I would walk the entire battlefield and look at the Mississippi River. For the life of me, I could not understand, nor could I find any reason published why General Pakenham landed *below* the American lines and marched to engage Jackson where he did. All Pakenham would have needed to do was sail right past the American line, sail five more miles, and he would have landed in an almost defenseless New

Orleans. The most that Jackson's troops could have done was wave at him as he passed by. He could have taken the city with almost no fight at all. Pakenham was, by no means, an inexperienced general. The British were winning in all other battles and skirmishes around New Orleans. So, why did Pakenham land and fight where he did? It maked no sense. It seemed impossible to me that the whole story was being told.

Let's look at some of the players on the American side to see what we know or *believe* that we know. First would have to be Andrew Jackson, the commander of the American forces at the Battle of New Orleans. Jackson was reported to be a 13 or 14-year-old courier for the American army during the war for independence. Reports say that Jackson was captured by the British and beaten, thereby accounting for Jackson's intense dislike of the British. It is unknown if this story is true, or a part of the legend/lore created about Jackson in later years. Jackson was a Freemason and a member of what would become Harmony Lodge No. 1 under the Grand Lodge of Tennessee. Jackson would become Grand Master of the Grand Lodge of Tennessee in 1822 and then elected President of the United States in 1829. Both events were likely the result of the notoriety and fame of Jackson following the Battle of New Orleans. Another politician and Freemason who played a role in the events was William C.C. Claiborne, the first governor of Louisiana in 1812. Claiborne was a member of Louisiana Lodge before the creation of the Grand Lodge of Louisiana, later joining Perfect Union Lodge No. 1. Claiborne's famous feud with the Lafitte brothers might have set into motion a chain of events that led to the outcome of the battle.

Then we have Jean and Pierre Lafitte; two brothers called pirates or buccaneers, depending on if one favored or did not favor them. Without question, the Battle of New Orleans could not have achieved the outcome that it did were not for the actions of Jean Lafitte. There is no record of Masonic membership of either of the Lafitte brothers. Then we have Captain Dominique Youx (sometimes spelled You), the commander of Jackson's cannons. Youx was a member of Charity Lodge No. 2 under the Grand Lodge of Louisiana and today has a lodge carrying his name. While it is not proven, Youx is often said to have been a cannoneer in Napoleon's army, moving to New Orleans at some point before the creation of the Grand Lodge in 1812. Another controversial and sometimes heatedly debated rumor about Youx is that he was the elder brother of Jean and Pierre Lafitte. The rumor says that the decision was made to keep Youx out of the questionable activities of his two younger brothers. The rumor goes on to say that this desire to keep the elder brother legitimate is the reason for the surname change. Regardless of the fact or fiction of this rumor, Youx was a liaison between the Lafitte brothers and Andrew Jackson.

The American government had given Andrew Jackson a daunting task. The Americans had noticed a significant buildup of British ships and troops in the Caribbean islands. An attack on America by the British was likely forthcoming. It was reasonable that the attack's goal would be to capture the valuable port of New Orleans. The problem for the Americans was that they had no idea when the attack would take place or where the British would land. Reports said the landing could be as far east as Mobile or west as Lafayette. Jackson based himself in New Orleans but realized he had nowhere near an appropriate troop size to defend such a large area. Another problem for Jackson was that he was extremely low on both gunpowder and flints. He simply did not have enough men to defend the area, and even if he did have the men, the gunpowder and flint shortage would render any defense futile. Jackson was not in good shape.

At the same time, Governor Claiborne was having different problems in New Orleans. Claiborne was shocked by what he felt was the lawlessness of the Creole population in New Orleans. The tolerance and even support of the citizens towards the smuggling operations of the Lafitte brothers confused and frustrated Claiborne. His disapproving attitude towards the Creoles made him unpopular in the city. Regardless, Claiborne was determined to clean up the city, and he felt the first place to start was with the Lafitte brothers. Claiborne ordered wanted posters to be placed all over New Orleans (at that time, limited to what is today the French Quarter). The posters offered a $500 reward for anyone delivering the Lafitte brothers to Claiborne. The following week, a new set of wanted posters were hanging all over the city. These posters offered a $1,000 reward for anyone who could deliver Claiborne to the Lafitte brothers in Barataria Bay. Claiborne was said to be livid. He was outraged by what he considered to be an audacious insult. Claiborne was more determined than ever to capture the Lafittes. It is not certain, however, if Claiborne's hostile feelings for the Lafittes were reciprocated. It is possible that the Lafittes were more dismissive of Claiborne and were only poking fun at him for their amusement. Regardless of how the Lafitte brothers felt about Claiborne, they should have taken him more seriously. The authorities captured Pierre Lafitte on a trip to New Orleans. He was placed in the jail of the Cabildo.[1]

Around the same time as the capture of Pierre Lafitte, visitors arrived at the Lafitte hideout in Barataria Bay.[2] The British had come calling with an offer for Jean Lafitte. They told Lafitte that they knew of his dislike for the government and asked for help. They explained their plan of attacking New Orleans but said they needed a map to navigate the tricky waterways leading into the city. In return for his help, the British offered payment and turning a blind eye to Lafitte's activities in the area. Lafitte reportedly asked about the outcome if he refused the offer. He was told that the British would find their own way into the city, and as they passed Lafitte's base, they would turn their guns on him. Lafitte agreed to the offer.

Wholly objective and reliable accounts of Jean Lafitte are difficult to find. A common opinion is that he was a vain man skilled at business but intensely disliked being challenged or questioned. The threat following the British offer must not have set well with Lafitte. He was also not at all happy about his brother sitting in the jail of the Cabildo. Lafitte had some past dealings with the Louisiana Secretary of State and contacted him about the British offer. Lafitte said that he would provide all the information the British gave him if Claiborne compensated him and released his brother from jail. Claiborne flatly refused. He said that he did not believe that Lafitte had any information of any value and that his brother would remain in jail. Claiborne added that soon, Jean

Lafitte would be joining his brother. Undaunted, Lafitte turned in another direction. He contacted Dominique Youx with information to pass on to Andrew Jackson. Lafitte made Youx the same offer that he made to Claiborne but added something extra. When Youx initially contacted Jackson about the offer, Jackson was not impressed. He felt that Lafitte could not be trusted. Youx assured Jackson that Lafitte's offer was legitimate and added the "extra" enticement. Youx told Jackson that Lafitte had an ample supply of gunpowder and flints that he would include in his offer if Jackson accepted. That tipped the scales for Jackson. He agreed to meet Lafitte, and the meeting was reportedly held at what is today The Old Absinthe House on Bourbon Street. The building was then Lafitte's importing firm (smugglings operation) in the heart of the French Quarter. Jackson agreed to the offer and then went to see Claiborne about the release of Pierre Lafitte.

The meeting between Andrew Jackson and William Claiborne concerning the release of Pierre Lafitte is a matter of pure speculation as to exactly what was said between the two. All that is known for sure is that Jackson asked for the release of Lafitte, and Claiborne refused. Given the fiery temper of both men, it can be assumed that some sharp words were exchanged, but the outcome was final. Claiborne would not release Pierre Lafitte. Jackson had no authority to order the release of Lafitte as he was being held on state charges. So, what was Jackson going to do? He needed the powder and flints to have any hope of success against the British. He had also already given his agreement to Jean Lafitte's offer. Claiborne had placed Jackson in an extremely difficult position.

The problem for Jackson concerning Pierre Lafitte, however, "solved itself" several days later. According to the newspapers of the day, Lafitte "escaped" from the jail of the Cabildo. No details have ever been published about *how* this "escape" was accomplished. All we know for sure is that Pierre Lafitte escaped and rejoined his brother in Barataria Bay. Jackson received the information about the British attack and all the gunpowder and flints he needed. So, without any evidence to support this statement, I'm going to venture a guess that Pierre Lafitte had some help in his escape. I suggest that the jailer, who was a Mason, went to Lafitte's jail cell, unlocked the cell door, and told him something along the lines of, "Get out of here. Your friends are waiting for you outside." Nothing else makes sense. The Cabildo was not a place from which people escaped. Anyone who has seen the jail of the Cabildo realizes why no one had escaped before this event. Without question, Jackson would not have received the information on the British, the gunpowder, or the flints if Pierre Lafitte had remained in jail. Where history remains silent, logic must fill in the gaps.

Andrew Jackson was in a far better position than before he met with Jean Lafitte. But problems remained. He knew the attack would come directly to New Orleans, but he did not know which route the British would take into the city. Jackson sent word to all the troops stationed along the Gulf Coast to return immediately to New Orleans. It was time for Jackson to devise a plan to defend the city. Jackson and his military command are often said to have met at Maspero's Coffee House on Chartres Street (but it can't be proven). The details of the meeting are as sketchy as the location.

Shortly before Christmas of 1814, the British warships were at the mouth of the Mississippi River. Jackson had begun his defense of New Orleans by building up the levee at the Rodriguez Canal. Several skirmishes with the British took place, mainly on the west bank of the Mississippi. None of these battles ended well for the Americans. At this time, a single American schooner, the *USS Carolina*, under the command of J. D. Henley (rumored, but never proven to be a Freemason) sailed out to engage the British. The *Carolina* fired on the British warships. Return fire from the British quickly set the *Carolina* on fire, and the bulk of the crew, including Henley, were captured. The *Carolina* exploded and sank. This is the thumbnail, generally accepted history of the events just before the final Battle of New Orleans. When we stop and consider the events, serious questions of logic arise that are unanswered in historical accounts.

Why were the American forces only successful against the British in the final battle? Why would a woefully under-gunned single schooner sail out to engage a fleet of British warships? Was Henley suicidal? Why did Jackson select the Rodriguez Canal to place all his troops to defend New Orleans? And finally, why in the world did Pakenham land his ships just *below* the Rodriguez Canal and march right into the American defenses when he could have landed *anywhere* else and had little to no resistance in capturing New Orleans? These questions are not answered in historical accounts.

Let's look at the situation through the eyes of a historian who must use logic and supposition to fill in the holes where evidence does not exist. To start with, the final battle's location at the Rodriguez Canal is now the town of Chalmette. It was such a decisive American victory that it overshadowed everything else about the events. The Americans did not see themselves as lucky to have won but as an invincible force that could not possibly lose regardless of the opponent. Jackson, Youx, and the Lafitte brothers became superstars with songs, stories, and legends built around them. But the ignored questions surrounding the events need to be answered, and the thin, unsupported rumors must be looked at harder. For example, J.D. Henley's actions with the *Carolina* are astonishing. What did he hope to gain? Why would any responsible commander take a ship that he knew had no chance of inflicting any serious damage into such an attack? He must have known the only possible outcome. Yet, he risked the lives of all his men and the ship for nothing. Or is that true? There is a completely unproven rumor that has floated around for many years. It is wholly discounted in most accounts as it may take something away from the invincible status of the American army. Let's look at it.

Andrew Jackson held a planning meeting of his military commanders. It can be logically assumed that Henley was present. The rumor exists that Jackson knew the danger facing New Orleans and that the most defendable route into New Orleans was through the Rodriguez Canal. Jackson knew that the location was perfect. With the river on one side and a swamp on the other, the British would be forced into a bottleneck and, by necessity, march across an open field with no cover. The American troops, however, would be protected by a reinforced levee. Jackson knew this was his choice for the battle, but how could he get the British to come to his party?

Jackson sought to devise a plan where the British would want to use this route for their attack on New Orleans. It is here that Henley is said to have presented a fascinating suggestion. Henley would take the *Carolina* out and attack the British warships. The British would quickly overpower the *Carolina* and capture the crew. As was their standard practice, they would interrogate the captain. One of the questions would be about the American defenses around New Orleans. Henley would then do something completely unthinkable and unbelievable for an officer and a gentleman of that time. He would lie. Henley would tell the British that the Americans were long expecting an attack on New Orleans, and the city was heavily defended by all routes, except for one. He would then hesitate and decline to give more information. Upon pressure, Henley would tell the British that the only lightly defended route into New Orleans was through the Chalmette Plantation across the Rodriguez Canal. Instead of telling the British of the only weak link in the American defenses, he told them the very route of the *only* defended one.

Of course, Jackson would have no way of knowing if the British would fall for this ruse. But what else could he do? He had one shot, and this seemed to be the best idea to get the British where he wanted them. He had only one backup plan. He was not going to allow the British to capture New Orleans. If the British did sail right past the American lines, Jackson had a small group of men stationed all around the city with only one job — burn the city to the ground.

Is any of this provable fact? Much of it is not. This paper should be read as only an examination of things unproven and even undocumented in Louisiana history. It is a theory based on a basic understanding of events. But, as we all know, the British did land below the Rodriguez Canal, and the outcome of the battle went down as one of the most significant wins for the American army. These are the facts. The unanswered question remains why.

By the way, I skimmed over one part of this story. I mentioned that the jailer guarding Pierre Lafitte in the Cabildo was a Mason. That's not conjecture. That's a fact. He was the one who seemed to have put doing what was necessary for the "greater good" ahead of what was the technical law. He was a man who was concerned with doing what was right, not easy, or safe. In fact, if it were not for that jailer, we can look at the Battle of New Orleans with a very different ending. I cannot reasonably see any scenario with a good outcome if Pierre Lafitte had not "escaped." The "escape" of Pierre Lafitte allowed everything else to happen. I firmly believe that the forgotten hero of the Battle of New Orleans was that jailer. The jailer was not only a Mason but would end up serving as Grand Master of the Grand Lodge of Louisiana and play a rather significant role in Texas Freemasonry. The young jailer's name is John Henry Holland. Most Worshipful Brother Holland had a long history of doing what he felt was *right* rather than what was popular, advantageous to him personally, or technically *proper*. He realized that sometimes we need to step up and get things done that we know need to be done. He was a man of action. He was the true definition of a Masonic leader. It is most fitting that a Mason of such honor, integrity, and courage would be the one to issue the warrant for the first lodge in Texas.

Notes:

1. In the days of the Spanish rule of Louisiana, the Cabildo was the Spanish city hall of New Orleans. It today serves as a Louisiana State Museum. The Cabildo is next to the St. Louis Cathedral across from Jackson Square.

2. Barataria Bay is in the Gulf of Mexico near southeastern Louisiana, near Grand Isle and Grand Terre.

About The Author

Michael R. Poll (1954 - present) is the owner of Cornerstone Book Publishers and former editor of the *Journal of The Masonic Society*. He is a Fellow and Past President of The Masonic Society, a Fellow of the Philalethes Society, a Fellow of the Maine Lodge of Research, Member of the Society of Blue Friars, and Full Member of the Texas Lodge of Research.

A New York Times Bestselling writer and publisher, he is a prolific writer, editor, and publisher of Masonic and esoteric books. He is also the host of the YouTube channel "New Orleans Scottish Rite College." As time permits, he travels and speaks on the history of Freemasonry, with a particular focus on the early history of the Scottish Rite.

He was born in New Orleans, LA and lives a peaceful life with his wife and two sons.

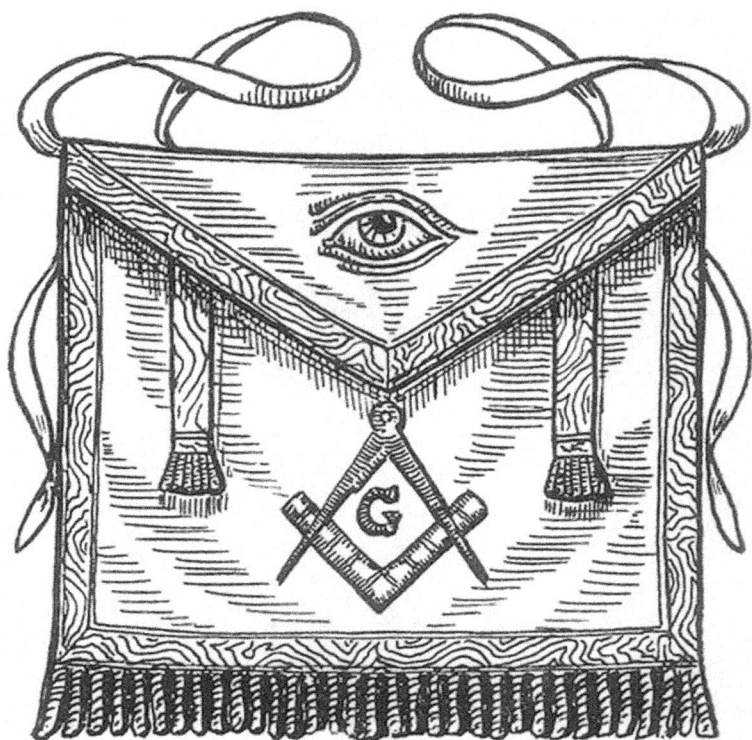

More Masonic Books from Cornerstone

In His Own (w)Rite
by Michael R. Poll
6×9 Softcover 176 pages
ISBN: 1613421575

Seeking Light
The Esoteric Heart of Freemasonry
by Michael R. Poll
6×9 Softcover 156 pages
ISBN: 1613422571

Measured Expectations
The Challenges of Today's Freemasonry
by Michael R. Poll
6×9 Softcover 180 pages
ISBN: 978-1613422946

A Masonic Evolution
The New World of Freemasonry
by Michael R. Poll
6×9 Softcover 176 pages
ISBN: 978-1-61342-315-8

An Encyclopedia of Freemasonry
by Albert Mackey
Revised by William J. Hughan and Edward L. Hawkins
Foreword by Michael R. Poll
8.5 x 11, Softcover 2 Volumes 960 pages
ISBN 1613422520

Cornerstone Book Publishers
www.cornerstonepublishers.com

More Masonic Books from Cornerstone

Masonic Enlightenment
The Philosophy, History and Wisdom of Freemasonry
Edited by Michael R. Poll
6 x 9 Softcover 180 pages
ISBN 1887560750

The Bonseigneur Rituals
A Rare Collection of 18th Century New Orleans Ecossais Rituals
Edited by Gerry L. Prinsen
Foreword by Michael R. Poll
8x10 Softcover 2 volumes 574 pages
ISBN 1934935344

Our Stations and Places - Masonic Officer's Handbook
by Henry G. Meacham
Revised by Michael R. Poll
6 x 9 Softcover 164 pages
ISBN: 1887560637

Knights & Freemasons: The Birth of Modern Freemasonry
By Albert Pike & Albert Mackey
Edited by Michael R. Poll
Foreword by S. Brent Morris
6 x 9 Softcover 178 pages
ISBN 1887560661

Robert's Rules of Order: Masonic Edition
Revised by Michael R. Poll
6 x 9 Softcover 212 pages
ISBN 1887560076

Cornerstone Book Publishers
www.cornerstonepublishers.com

New Orleans Scottish Rite College

www.youtube.com/c/NewOrleansScottishRiteCollege

Clear, Easy to Watch
Scottish Rite and Craft Lodge
Video Education

www.ingramcontent.com/pod-product-compliance
Lightning Source LLC
Chambersburg PA
CBHW031125020426
42333CB00012B/238